Skills for Success

Working and studying in English

Donna Price-Machado
San Diego Community College District

CAMBRIDGE
UNIVERSITY PRESS

CAMBRIDGE UNIVERSITY PRESS
Cambridge, New York, Melbourne, Madrid, Cape Town, Singapore, São Paulo, Delhi

Cambridge University Press
32 Avenue of the Americas, New York, NY 10013–2473, USA

www.cambridge.org
Information on this title: www.cambridge.org/9780521657426

First published 1998
4th printing 2008

Printed in the United States of America

A catalog record for this publication is available from the British Library

ISBN 978-0-521-65742-6 Student's Book

Cover photography: (top) ©TSM/Jose L. Pelaez;
(bottom) COMSTOCK, INC./Michael Stuckey

Table of Contents

Scope and Sequence

Chapter	Workplace/Academic Behaviors (SCANS)	Functions
1 What Are Employers Looking For?	**Resources:** Allocating time to activities **Interpersonal:** Negotiating meanings of want ads **Information:** Analyzing and interpreting want ads **Systems:** Evaluating performance **Thinking Skills:** Describing events	Checking other people's understanding Checking one's own understanding
2 Building Self-Confidence	**Information:** Organizing information by ranking Using a graphic organizer to organize information **Thinking skills:** Using visuals to make predictions Applying rules to figure out correct spelling **Personal qualities:** Building self-esteem Assessing self accurately	Agreeing Disagreeing
3 Volunteering: On-the-Job Training	**Information:** Organizing information by clustering **Systems:** Monitoring and correcting pronunciation **Thinking skills:** Using want ads to make conclusions Figuring out meaning by using contextual clues	Expressing opinions Asking for repetition or clarification
4 Effective Job Applications	**Resources:** Acquiring and using job applications **Information:** Organizing information in chronological order **Systems:** Understanding job application forms Monitoring and correcting pronunciation **Thinking skills:** Using clues to make predictions Paraphrasing **Personal qualities:** Taking responsibility	Giving suggestions
5 Successful Job Interviews	**Information:** Using a graphic organizer to organize information **Systems:** Understanding social systems Evaluating performance **Thinking skills:** Deciding best responses to difficult questions **Personal qualities:** Assessing self accurately	Restating for clarification

Team Activity	Grammar	Assessment Test (in Teacher's Support Materials)
Brainstorming Cooperative learning: Doing a specified task	Participial adjectives	page T-56
Cooperative learning: Jigsaw reading Role play	Common spelling rules	page T-58
Cooperative learning: Jigsaw reading Clustering	Present perfect vs. past tense	page T-60
Cooperative learning: Doing a specified task Round-robin reading	Capitalization, punctuation, past tense on application forms	page T-62
Cooperative learning: Jigsaw reading Interviewing	Gerunds as subjects	page T-64

Scope and Sequence

Chapter	Workplace/Academic Behaviors (SCANS)	Functions
6 Small Talk at the Water Cooler	**Resources:** Allocating time to an activity **Information:** Using categories to organize information **Systems:** Evaluating performance Understanding social systems **Thinking skills:** Using visuals to make predictions **Personal qualities:** Assessing self accurately	Ending a conversation politely
7 Improving Relationships at Work	**Information:** Interpreting bar graphs **Basic skills:** Computing percentages **Thinking skills:** Reasoning by using contextual clues Solving problems Organizing bar graphs Paraphrasing	Giving advice
8 Handling Criticism	**Systems:** Using flowcharts Evaluating performance Monitoring and correcting pronunciation **Thinking skills:** Reasoning by using contextual clues Paraphrasing Solving a problem **Personal qualities:** Assessing self accurately	Offering and accepting apologies
9 Having a Positive Attitude	**Systems:** Monitoring and correcting pronunciation **Thinking skills:** Listing purposes of business letters Solving problems Paraphrasing **Personal qualities:** Assessing self accurately Building self-esteem	Bringing other people into a conversation Expressing gratitude
10 Writing at Work	**Interpersonal:** Negotiating clarity of memos **Systems:** Writing memos and e-mail **Thinking skills:** Predicting meaning from titles Paraphrasing Applying rules to analyze memos	Giving instructions

Team Activity	Grammar	Assessment Test (in Teacher's Support Materials)
Brainstorming Round table Cooperative learning: Jigsaw reading	Question formation	page T-66
Quick write Cooperative learning: Jigsaw reading Doing a specified task	Common modal auxiliaries: **should, ought to, had better, would, would rather**	page T-68
Round table Cooperative learning: Jigsaw reading Doing a specified task	Negative questions	page T-70
Cooperative learning: Jigsaw reading Role play	Subject-verb agreement	page T-72
Cooperative learning: Doing a specified task Jigsaw reading	Active and passive voice	page T-74

All chapters of *Skills for Success* integrate the following SCANS competencies and skills.

Resources:
Using materials such as a dictionary and a thesaurus

Interpersonal:
Participating as a member of a team
Teaching others new skills

Information:
Interpreting and communicating information

Systems:
Monitoring and correcting performance

Technology:
Selecting technology *(Online!)*

Basic skills:
Reading, writing, listening, speaking

Personal qualities:
Demonstrating sociability

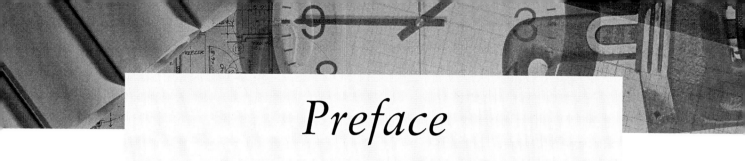

Preface

BRIEF DESCRIPTION AND RATIONALE

Skills for Success integrates English language instruction with the teaching of the competencies essential for succeeding on the job or in an academic setting. This theme-based and student-centered text gets students reading, talking, and writing about such topics as building self-confidence, handling criticism, managing a successful job interview, and making small talk with colleagues. All content and activities in *Skills for Success* are informed by the SCANS competencies, developed by the Secretarys Commission on Achieving Necessary Skills. This U.S. government commission has attempted to define the "soft skills" necessary in the workplace, such as working in teams, correcting performance, solving problems, and using technology, all with the goal of helping people to become job-ready in a shorter period of time and to maintain and thrive in their existing jobs. These workplace behaviors are also expected in academic settings.

PHILOSOPHY AND APPROACH

Skills for Success is a theme-based, integrated-skills approach that encourages lively student interaction through cooperative learning techniques. The chapters are organized following the basic steps of a well-organized lesson plan. Material is introduced in cycles of preparation, practice, and evaluation that integrate the skills of listening, speaking, reading, writing, and basic math. Each chapter has the dual purpose of building language skills and developing an awareness of appropriate workplace and academic behavior.

AUDIENCE AND LEVEL

Skills for Success can be used by a wide range of students who are preparing to work or who already work or study in an English-speaking environment, including those attending non-credit ESL classes, two- and four-year colleges, intensive English programs, vocational ESL classes, and on-site workplace programs. Native speakers in adult basic education classes will also find this book useful. The level ranges from intermediate to advanced.

CONTENT AND SKILLS

Skills for Success integrates speaking, listening, reading, writing, and math in a variety of student-focused activities, such as jigsaw, round table, and clustering. Grammar and vocabulary are presented in the context of topics related to the world of work. All content and activities integrate the

SCANS competencies and foundation skills. In addition, the instructional approach of each chapter meets the standards of the California State Model Standards for Adult ESL programs. In terms of the standards developed by the Comprehensive Adult Student Assessment System (CASAS), the skill level of the text is equivalent to Student Performance Levels (SPL) 4–6, Low Intermediate through Advanced, and to scores 200–235 on the CASAS scale.

SCANS

Skills for Success integrates the skills and competencies described in the SCANS report. The report outlines two categories of abilities that people must develop if they are to succeed in high-performance workplaces. The first category covers foundation skills, including basic skills (speaking, listening, reading, writing, and math); thinking skills (creative thinking, decision-making, problem-solving, reasoning, and knowing how to learn); and personal qualities (responsibility, self-esteem, social skills, self-management, and integrity).

The second category describes competencies that include working well in teams, using resources, acquiring and evaluating data, and understanding and using technology. A chart showing the SCANS competencies taught in every chapter appears in the Teacher's Manual.

FEATURES

- All chapters focus on both academic and work skills, thus appealing to a wide audience.

- Skill level is equivalent to CASAS Student Performance Levels 4–6. The instructional approaches meet the instructional standards of the California State Model Standards for Adult ESL programs.

- SCANS competencies (workplace know-how) are interwoven in all content and exercises.

- Student-focused communicative activities use a variety of techniques to expand students' understanding of content and to develop their language skills.

- Activities encourage team interactions typical of many workplaces and academic settings.

- Readings from authentic newspaper articles highlight workplace issues.

- **Online!** sections give students addresses for finding more information on the content of each chapter.

- **How to Say It** sections teach students common expressions needed in academic and work settings, such as those used to clarify meaning, to respond to criticism, or to close a conversation.

- Chapters may be used independently, in any order.

ORGANIZATION

Every chapter of *Skills for Success* includes the following major sections:

Objectives. The objectives show students what they will learn. The objectives also serve as a model of an agenda, an organizational system used in the workplace, and one of the SCANS competencies.

Workplace Know-How. This section provides a brief description of the SCANS foundation skills and competencies that students will focus on in the chapter.

Talk About It! This brief, conversational ice-breaker gets students to focus on the chapter topic by activating their own knowledge about and experience with it.

Take It Down! This section includes a dictation that provides a summary of what students will learn in each chapter and integrates the grammar focus of the chapter.

Read About It! Students read an article or section from an authentic newspaper that focuses on an important workplace issue.

Practical Grammar. Grammar, taught in the context of the chapter themes, presents important, practical structures in a meaningful, communicative way. Explanations integrate simple checks (**Can you do it?**) to ensure that students grasp each concept. Additional exercises provide ample practice.

Write It Up! This section gives students the opportunity to develop such prewriting and writing skills as clustering, semantic mapping using graphic organizers, summarizing, and composing business letters and e-mail messages.

Check It! Students reflect on what they have learned in each chapter and complete Academic and Work Skills Checklists.

Additionally, the Teacher's Manual provides an Assessment Test for every chapter to document students' progress and give them input on what they have learned.

Acknowledgments

Skills for Success is dedicated to all students who juggle work schedules, child-care needs, and health and transportation difficulties to come to school to enrich and improve their lives. It is also dedicated to the many ESL instructors who spend hours on lesson plans and in classrooms and who give unstintingly of their energy, creativity, and time for their students. I began work on this book in 1996, when, after searching for appropriate textbooks for my ESL and vocational ESL courses, I started to piece together the lesson plans that formed the basis for my classes.

The development of a textbook is a long and complex process, and many individuals contribute along the way. There are so many people who have been so generous to me over the years, that I do not even know where to begin. A few words in a preface do not capture the quality nor the extent of my gratitude, but these acknowledgments offer me a place to register my sincere appreciation to the many people who have taught me most of what I know about second-language teaching, provided tireless and seemingly endless staff development resources, all the while supporting my students and me while I was writing *Skills for Success*: Gretchen Bitterlin, Leann Howard, Autumn Keltner, Dr. Ann Johns, Rod Smith, President of Continuing Education and Frances Lee, Dean of Continuing Education, both of San Diego Community College District. I would also like to extend my gratitude to Ann Marie Damrau for her encouragement, friendship, patience, and collaboration.

I am grateful to the members of CATESOL for giving me opportunities to learn about all levels of ESL and for providing a forum for all instructors to exchange ideas and techniques. I thank the people at CASAS for their expertise on testing and assessment, which I hope is reflected in the pages of *Skills for Success*. I want to add a special note of thanks to Brigitte Marshall for her dedication to the ESL field, willingness to travel, creation of newsletters, and for sharing her expertise on SCANS.

Skills for Success benefited from the many suggestions and candid remarks of consultants and reviewers in programs around the country. I learned a lot from the following colleagues, who read and in some cases reread various drafts of the manuscript:

Elinor T. Abdulla
University of Texas – Pan American
English Language Institute, Edinburg, Texas

Sally Bates
Long Beach School for Adults, Long Beach, California

Gretchen Bitterlin
San Diego Community College District, San Diego, California

Joann Crandall
University of Maryland Baltimore County, Baltimore, Maryland

Frank Elsea
Lindsey Hopkins Technical Education Center (DCPS),
Miami, Florida

Susan Gaer
Rancho Santiago College, Santa Ana, California

M. Maureen Garry
Milwaukee Area Technical College, Milwaukee, Wisconsin

Allene Grognet
Center for Applied Linguistics, Sarasota, Florida

Kathryn R. Hamilton
Elk Grove Adult Education, Sacramento, California

Leann B. Howard
formerly San Diego Community College District,
San Diego, California

Joyce Inch
Long Beach School for Adults, Long Beach, California

Brigitte Marshall
California State Department of Social Services
Refugee Programs Bureau

Monica Oliva
Miami-Dade Public Schools, Miami, Florida

Sylvia G. Ramirez
MiraCosta Adult Learning Center, Carlsbad, California

One can never anticipate all the twists and turns that a project may take, and I could not have predicted that I would ever hold the finished copy of *Skills for Success* that you have in your hands right now. I would like to thank a number of very skilled publishing professionals for helping me to make it happen. Without the insight, expertise, and encouragement of Marian Wassner, *Skills for Success* could not have been published. Before writing this book, I had no idea what editors really do – Marian not only had the ability to see creativity and purpose in the lesson plans that I originally submitted, but understood my vision for a book and collaborated with me so that I would achieve it. In addition to learning about what does and does not constitute a chapter head structure, I have grown to trust Marian as a devoted publisher and friend. I would also like to express my sincere appreciation to Debbie Brennan, Steve Debow, Maria Garcia, and Gordon Johnson for their unwavering support of *Skills for Success* through a very difficult transition in their own lives. Tina Carver believed in me and persuaded me to bring my materials to St. Martin's Press in the first place.

At Cambridge University Press, Mary Vaughn and John Borrelli have worked closely with me in putting the finishing touches on *Skills for Success* and spreading its goals to the teaching community. Thank you, everyone!

Finally, I thank my husband, Sergio Machado, for helping me with the computer and for letting me ignore him for over a year.

D.P.M.

7/98

To *the student*

Students often ask, "How long will it take me to learn English?" A good book and a good teacher will help, but students themselves must take some of the responsibility. Here are several things you can do to facilitate learning while you are using *Skills for Success*.

1. **Keep a vocabulary notebook.**

   Buy a small memo book. As you read the articles in each chapter, write down new vocabulary words along with a brief definition of each word. Periodically go through your notebook to review the words. You will be surprised at how many of the words you learn this way will carry over to your college or vocational life.

2. **Keep a grammar notebook.**

   Keep track of the grammar rules you learned in the *Practical Grammar* section of each chapter. You will see an improvement in your writing as you become aware of the specific mistakes you are making.

3. **Do the checklists at the end of every chapter.**

   The checklists give you the opportunity to reflect on what you have learned in each chapter. In this way you can evaluate your own progress and achievements and learn the language to describe them. One common question prospective employers often ask students during a job interview is, "What do you learn in your English class?" The checklists will help you answer that question fully.

4. **Monitor your use of English.**

   Once or twice a month, fill out the *Monitoring Your English* form on the next page. Think about where you used your English, who you spoke to, why you used it, and if you had any problems. Work on your weaknesses and be proud of your strengths.

5. **Keep a log book.**

   In business, employees often use log books to communicate with the next shift. Workers write what they did that day. In college, students frequently write in journals. Keeping a log book will help your fluency in writing and will give you the opportunity to express what you have accomplished in class. Use the log book topics listed after this section (see page xvii) as a guide.

6. Chart your progress on chapter tests.

An Assessment Test is provided for every chapter. Chart your progress on the Progress Graph that appears after this section, on page xviii.

7. Practice working effectively in teams.

In college and business, you will work in teams. One of the biggest concerns of employers today is the need to find workers who can get along with each other. When there are interpersonal problems, productivity and morale decrease. The activities in *Skills for Success* give you many opportunities to work in teams. Take advantage of your time in class to figure out ways to work effectively with people who are different from you.

MONITORING YOUR ENGLISH

Being aware of when you use English and the problems you have in certain situations will help you monitor and correct your own performance. Once or twice a month, fill out this chart. Then discuss it with your teacher and classmates. What does it tell you about your strengths and weaknesses?

I used my English . . .

Where were you?	With whom did you communicate?	What did you communicate about?	What problems did you have communicating?
_____	_____	_____	_____
_____	_____	_____	_____
_____	_____	_____	_____
_____	_____	_____	_____
_____	_____	_____	_____
_____	_____	_____	_____
_____	_____	_____	_____
_____	_____	_____	_____
_____	_____	_____	_____

Log book topics

At least twice a week, answer any or all of these questions in your log books.

IN CLASS

1. What did you learn today that will help you in your job or personal life?

2. What did you like or dislike about the lesson?

3. What happened with your team or partner?

4. Did you do anything today to help someone in class? What did you do?

IN THE COMMUNITY

1. Are you a U.S. citizen? Did you register to vote? Did you vote?

2. Are you involved in your community? Explain what you do.

3. Are you taking a citizenship class?

IN YOUR CHILD'S SCHOOL

1. Have you gone to your child's school?

2. Did you volunteer to help?

3. Do you read to your child?

AT WORK

1. Did you get a job recently?

2. Did you do something special at work, such as get an award or a promotion?

IN YOUR EDUCATION

1. Did you enter a job-training class?

2. Are you taking other classes? Are you taking college classes?

Progress Graph for chapter tests

Chart your progress on the chapter tests. Each time you take a test, mark your score on the graph. Then connect your scores to make a line graph.

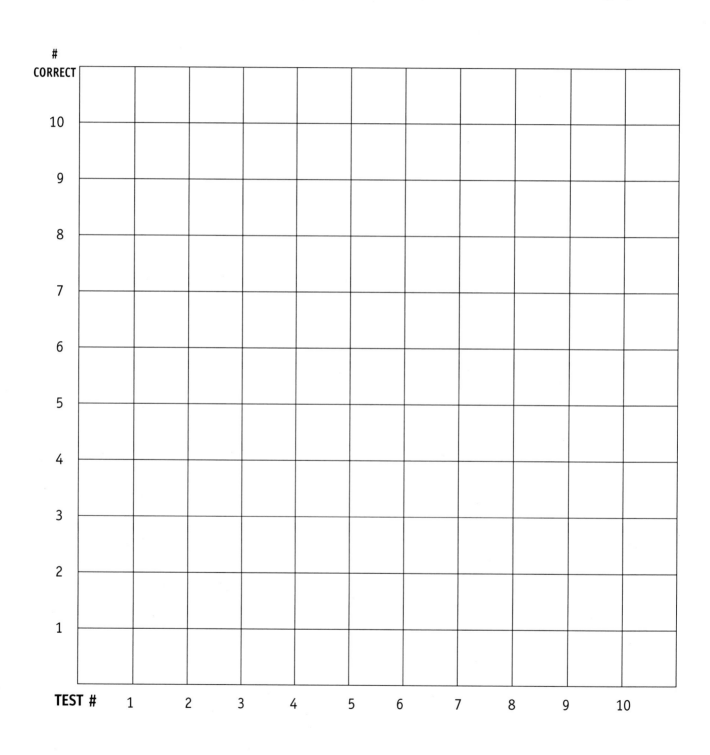

Skills for Success

Working and studying in English

Chapter 1

What Are Employers Looking For?

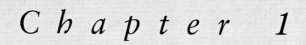
OBJECTIVES

By the end of this chapter, you will be able to:

■ Interpret and communicate information from want ads.

■ Describe activities and procedures you do in class and explain how they compare with what employers want you to do.

■ Demonstrate your ability to work effectively in teams to complete certain tasks.

■ Use participial adjectives to describe personal and work qualities.

■ Write a paragraph describing an event.

■ Revise and edit your own and a classmate's paragraph.

■ Use appropriate language to check someone's comprehension.

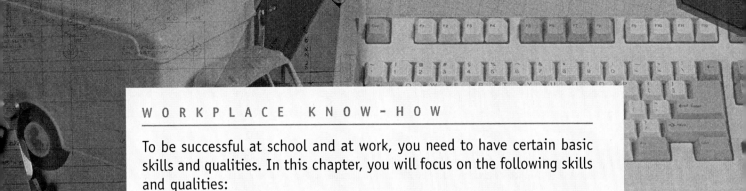

To be successful at school and at work, you need to have certain basic skills and qualities. In this chapter, you will focus on the following skills and qualities:

1. Analyzing and interpreting information
2. Thinking creatively
3. Using your time efficiently
4. Working on a team
5. Negotiating meaning

Talk about it!

1. Did you ever apply for a job from the help-wanted ads? Did you get the job?

2. If you are from another country, do the newspapers in your country contain a help wanted section? What are some of the similarities and differences between the help-wanted ads here and in your country?

Take it down!

Your teacher will dictate a paragraph that covers the content and the grammar in this chapter. First, write what you hear. Then check it by using the Dictation Revision Form on the back inside cover.

_____

_____

_____

_____

_____

◈ Read about it!

PREPARATION: **Brainstorming**

Brainstorming is a good way to come up with new ideas or a solution to a problem. When a group of people brainstorm, they call out or write down all their ideas about a topic or a problem. With a partner or in small groups, make a list of specific things employers are looking for in all people who apply for jobs. Share your list with other groups. What qualities were mentioned most often?

_____

_____

_____

PRACTICE: **Interpreting and communicating information in want ads**

A. Read the ads. What are employers looking for? Read the following want ads for general meaning. Don't try to understand every word.

a. **Nursing**

CNA's

FT, CNA's needed for day & eve. shifts. Must be team player, w/positive outlook, strong skills, & exp. in SNF. Come and join a winning team! Outstanding salary, bonus, & benefits! Xlnt staff-to-patient ratios! Apply in person to:

Denise Frank, DON
Hillsdale Nursing & Rehab Ctr.
123 E. Elizabeth St.
No phone calls.   EOE.

b. Restaurant

Waitress, hostess, busboy

M/F, part-time, honest, hardworking team players needed. Neat appearance. Friendly. Apply between 2-3.

1251 13th Ave. No phone calls please.

c.

The Shore View Hotel is looking for bright, energetic & experienced team players to join a great hotel staff. Competitive salary & benefits. Bilingual a plus. We have the following positions available:

- ♦ Coffee cart attendant
- ♦ Restaurant servers/hostess
- ♦ Bartender
- ♦ Bellman/driver w/cls B lic.

Please apply in person at:
1800 Frontage Road

e.

Receptionist

Busy Dallas dental office. Bilingual a plus. Must be energetic and reliable with a great attitude. Includes heavy filing, photocopying, correspondence, & repetitive misc. tasks. Mac experience desired. Apply in person at:

316 St. Michael's Way
or call Jean, 555-1000

d.

Retail

SALESPERSON

Join our company for part-time sales opportunities in the Fort Worth area. We are looking for team members who are bilingual (Spanish/English) and are available to work flexible hours (between 10:00 A.M. and 7:00 P.M. Sunday through Saturday). Salary: $5.75 per hour + incentives. Apply at:

Marshall's Furniture

5455 S. Elk Drive, 3rd floor
Fort Worth
between 10:00 A.M.-12:00 noon
2:00 P.M.-4:00 P.M.

or call for an appointment
555-1212

f.

Quality Electronics   555-7890

TEST TECHNICIAN

Requires AS degree in Electronics with 2-4 years experience or equivalent. Must have ability to troubleshoot and repair RF electronic equipment. Team players. Xlnt co. pd. benefits.

Fax résumé to 555-7892.

Automotive Technician
Lube technician

Full-time positions. Great entry-level position for a self-motivated, quality oriented person with the right attitude.

Apply Mon-Fri 8 A.M.-5 P.M. to Dan Moultin
James Dean Cadillac
4275 Wornall Rd.
Lawrence, Kansas

g.

B. Find the ads. Write the letter of the advertisement for each job.

1. __f, g__ trades
2. _____ clerical fields
3. _____ medical fields
4. _____ retailing fields
5. _____ food service fields
6. _____ hotel industry

C. Work together. With a partner, answer these questions about the want ads.

1. There are a few qualities that many of the ads have in common. What are they?

    _____

2. a. What very important skill is mentioned in the ad for the test technician job?

    _____

    b. Can you explain what this word means?

    _____

    c. Do you ever use that skill in this class? When?

    _____

3. Find an ad that interests you. What do we do in this class that prepares you for that job?

    _____

    _____

4. Imagine that you're going for an interview for the job that interests you. What can you tell the interviewer if he/she asks, "Is there anything you want to tell me about yourself?"

    _____

    _____

    _____

5. Write two or three sentences explaining why you think your instructor gave you this exercise to do.

    _____

    _____

    _____

EVALUATION: **Monitor and correct your work**

Discuss your answers with the whole class.

A. Search. For more about what employers are looking for, look for these addresses on the Internet or search on your own.

- Essential skills for success:
  http://www.umr.edu/~megbrady/scansskills.html

- Job skills sought by employers:
  describing yourself: Lesson 9
  http://www.otan.dni.us./webfarm/emailproject/
    rancho/intro.htm

B. Report. After you find the addresses, tell your classmates or write a brief paragraph about three or four of the skills most in demand by employers.

N O T E

If you don't have a computer or cannot get on the Internet at home, you can:

1. Go to a public library near your home or school. Libraries usually have free Internet access.

2. Find out if you can get on the Internet at your school. Schools often have Internet access.

3. Ask a friend if you can use his or her computer to get on the Internet.

Practical grammar: Adjectives that look like verbs

USAGE AND FORM

Many of you have already applied for jobs. One question interviewers often ask is, "What can you tell me about yourself that isn't in your résumé?" It's important to talk honestly about your strengths and weaknesses. Adjectives will help you describe experiences and events and how you feel about them.

Look at the examples below and think about what the words in bold type have in common:

> I'm **organized**.
> I'm **interested** in learning new things.
> I'm **motivated**.
> I'm **excited** about working with computers
> I feel very **qualified** for this type of work.

Can you do it? With a partner, answer these questions.

1. What do the words in bold type have in common?

To describe the way people feel, use participial adjectives that end in **-ed**. These participial adjectives look like verbs in the regular past tense.

2. How do you know the words in bold type are not verbs in the past tense?

....

Look at this next set of examples and think about what the words in bold type have in common.

> Working with computers is **exciting**.
> My job is **interesting**.
> This task is **boring**.

Can you do it? With a partner, answer these questions.

1. What do the words in bold type have in common?

To describe an experience, an event, or an activity, use participial adjectives that end in **-ing**. These participial adjectives look like verbs in the present continuous tense.

2. How do you know the words in bold type are not verbs in the present continuous tense?

....

Compare each group of statements.

■ **bored, boring**

She is **bored**.	(You are describing the way she feels. Something is making her feel bored.)
The task is **boring**.	(You are describing a task or a characteristic of the task.)

■ **interested, interesting**

The student is **interested** in the lecture. (You are describing the way the student feels. Something in the lecture interests the student.)

This is an **interesting** class. (You are describing a characteristic of the class.)

Can you do it? With a partner, underline the adjectives that describe how people feel. Circle the adjectives that describe experiences or activities.

1. She's an experienced data-entry clerk.

2. Welding is very physically challenging.

3. The employees are motivated because they like their work.

4. Some people think assembly work is boring; other people never get bored doing that kind of work.

5. The student is satisfied with the report she wrote for her history class.

PRACTICE

A. Feelings or characteristics? With a group of three students, fill in the correct adjective. Discuss why you chose the answer you did. Ask yourselves: (1) Are we describing a person's feelings? (2) Are we describing the characteristics of a person or thing?

1. I was _____ at the job interview. (excited, exciting)

2. I heard some _____ news yesterday. (surprised, surprising)

3. The flight attendants were _____ after the trip. (exhausted, exhausting)

4. The foreman told an _____ story. (amused, amusing)

5. Were you _____ to learn more about computers after you used one for the first time? (motivated, motivating)

6. Speaking in front of a large group can be a _____ experience. (thrilled, thrilling)

7. The student is so _____ at that job. She keeps falling asleep. (bored, boring)

B. Describe your feelings and experiences. In teams of four, describe an experience you had and how you felt about it. First, each member should choose a job from the list below.

LEADER: You will be the first to speak. While your teammates are speaking, make sure everyone stays on task, that is, keeps to the topic. After each talk, make sure everyone asks the speaker a question.

TIMEKEEPER: Make sure everyone talks for at least two minutes but not more than three minutes. Watch the clock discreetly. (While you are speaking, the leader will be the timekeeper.)

REPORTER: Tell the whole class about one of your teammate's talks.

GRAMMAR COP: Politely correct students who use language incorrectly in their talks or their questions.

Next each member should choose a topic from the list below.

you went on a job interview	your job
you got hired for a job	your school
you got fired from a job	your family
you had an accident	your wedding
you took a trip	your child

Now take a few minutes to think about your topic. Look at the types of experiences listed below.

exciting	boring	frightening
amusing	exhausting	surprising
depressing	disappointing	annoying
frustrating		

What kind of experience did you have? How did you feel? Make some notes to use while you speak.

_____

_____

_____

_____

_____

Checking others' and your own understanding

In some situations, such as when you give directions or tell a story, you want to be sure the people listening to you understand what you are talking about. In addition, you may need to check with a speaker to be sure you understand what he/she is saying. Use these common expressions when you want to check others' or your own understanding:

1. Checking another person's understanding:

  Do you follow me?

  Are you with me so far?

  Be sure to ask if you have any questions.

  Have you got it?

  Can you repeat what I just told you? } appropriate to say to someone you are training or to a coworker

2. Checking your own understanding:

  Let me see if I've got that right.

  Let me see. First I have to . . .

  Let me repeat that.

Say It! Use one or more of these expressions while listening to your classmates talk about their experiences.

Now begin your talks. Remember the following rules:

■ Talk for 2–3 minutes.

■ Use participial adjectives in your talk.

■ Prepare a question to ask each teammate after his/her talk.

EVALUATION: **Monitor and correct your work**

Evaluate your own and your teammates' talks using the questions below. Rate each team member on a scale of 1–5 for each category on the Evaluation Sheet (5 = excellent; 1 = needs improvement).

Performance:

> Did the student do the assigned job?
> How well did he/she perform the job?

Presentation:

> Did the student talk for at least two minutes?
> How good was the talk?

Question:

> Did the student ask the person speaking a question?
> How good was the question?

Cooperation:

> Did the student participate in the activity and help others in the group?

Evaluation Sheet

Team #_____

Evaluation: 1–5
(5 = excellent; 1 = needs improvement)

JOB	NAME	PERFORMANCE	PRESENTATION	QUESTION	COOPERATION
Leader	_____	_____	_____	_____	_____
Timekeeper	_____	_____	_____	_____	_____
Reporter	_____	_____	_____	_____	_____
Grammar cop	_____	_____	_____	_____	_____

◆ Write it up!

PREPARATION: **Jotting down the details**

Write a paragraph about the same experience you described to your teammates. Before you begin, write answers to the following questions. These questions will help you remember important details to include in your paragraph.

1. When did it happen? _____
_____

2. Where did it happen? _____
_____

3. Who was with you when it happened? _____
_____

4. How did it happen? _____
_____

5. Why did you feel the way you described? _____
_____

6. Describe your feelings in detail. _____
_____

PRACTICE: **Writing a paragraph**

Using the answers from the previous exercise, write a paragraph on a separate piece of paper about the event you described to your teammates.

EVALUATION: **Monitor and correct your work**

After you finish writing the paragraph, give it to a classmate to read. Your classmate will evaluate your paragraph by completing the revision checklist on the next page.

Classmate Revision Checklist

WRITER'S NAME: _____

CHECKER'S NAME: _____

Circle *yes* or *no*.

1. Can you read the writer's handwriting?   YES   NO
   (If you circled *no*, ask the writer to rewrite it.)

2. Did you understand the events of the story?   YES   NO
   (If you circled *no*, explain to the writer what you
   didn't understand.)

3. Did the writer use any participial adjectives?   YES   NO
   Write one of them here. _____

4. Are all the verbs in the correct tense?   YES   NO
   (If you circled *no*, help the writer correct them.)

5. Are all the words spelled correctly?   YES   NO
   (If you circled *no*, help the writer make corrections.
   If you're not sure of the spelling, use a dictionary.)

6. Does every sentence begin with a capital letter?   YES   NO

7. Does every sentence end with a period?   YES   NO

8. Did you enjoy reading this paragraph?   YES   NO
   Why or why not? _____

After you correct your paper, recopy it or type it and hand it in. Your instructor will tell both you and the person who checked your paper if there are any problems with it.

 # Check it!

Put a checkmark next to each activity you accomplished in this chapter.

ACADEMIC SKILLS CHECKLIST

Did you . . .

_____ write new vocabulary words in a notebook?

_____ write new grammar rules in a notebook?

_____ interpret and communicate information from the want ads?

_____ describe an experience to your teammates using participial adjectives?

_____ write a paragraph about your experience?

_____ revise your paragraph with the help of a classmate?

_____ evaluate a classmate's paragraph using the revision checklist?

_____ use resources in the classroom, such as a dictionary or a thesaurus?

_____ use the Internet to get more information about the topic?

WORK SKILLS CHECKLIST

Did you . . .

_____ work effectively in your team?

_____ do the job that was assigned to you? What was that job?

_____

_____ allocate the time available for the task?

_____ assess the performance of your teammates?

_____ assess your own performance?

_____ use the computer (if available) to type your final paragraph?

_____ use expressions to check your own or your teammates' understanding? What is one expression you used?

_____

Chapter 2

Building Self-Confidence

By the end of this chapter, you will be able to:

■ Teach classmates information you acquired from an article.

■ Define self-confidence.

■ Identify some reasons why lack of self-confidence develops.

■ List general ways to increase self-confidence.

■ Describe your personal strengths and explain which of these strengths are important in your career field.

■ Write, revise, and edit a paragraph.

■ Use several rules for spelling common words correctly.

■ Use appropriate language to agree and disagree.

To be successful at school and at work, you need to have certain basic skills and qualities. In this chapter, you will focus on the following skills and qualities:

1. Analyzing and interpreting information

2. Identifying personal qualities

3. Organizing information

4. Ranking from the top in descending order

Talk about it!

1. How would you define self-confidence?

2. What are some ways people can increase their self-confidence?

Take it down!

Your teacher will dictate a paragraph that covers the content and the grammar in this chapter. First, write what you hear. Then check it by using the Dictation Revision Form on the back inside cover.

_____

_____

_____

_____

_____

◆ Read about it!

PREPARATION: **Using visuals to make predictions**

Being able to make predictions about the content of an article or other text will make you a better reader. Usually the title of the article, as well as its section titles, contain important clues about the topic. Examining illustrations or photos that accompany an article will also help you make accurate predictions about it.

In a group of four students, try to predict the content of the article by examining the pictures.

A. Read the list of words and match each word to the picture that it describes. Discuss the meanings of the words as you talk about the pictures. Use a dictionary if necessary.

optimistic	passive	isolated	proud
depressed	lonely	eager	unsure
independent	realistic		

B. What might have happened to the woman in the picture on the left? How did she lose her self-confidence? What can she do to get her self-confidence back?

C. What might have happened to the woman in the picture on the right? How did she increase her self-confidence?

Discuss your group's answers with the class.

A. Read the article. In your group of four students, number 1-4.

STUDENTS 1 AND 2:
Read the section **How does a lack of self-confidence develop?**

STUDENTS 3 AND 4:
Read the section **How to increase your self-confidence.**

What Is Self-Confidence?

Self-confidence primarily refers to having a positive and realistic perception of ourselves and our abilities. Self-confidence is characterized by: optimism, eagerness, pride, independence, trust, the ability to handle criticism, emotional maturity, and the ability to accurately assess our capabilities.

A lack of self-confidence, on the other hand, is characterized by: self-doubt, passivity, isolation, sensitivity to criticism, distrust, depression, and feelings of inferiority and being unloved.

How does a lack of self-confidence develop?

1. Negative life experiences at home, in school, or on the job can cause you to develop feelings of inferiority and hopelessness. For example, when you were growing up your parents might have been unable to provide a healthy and supportive environment. Perhaps they were critical, demanding and/or overprotective of you. As a result, you develop negative perceptions of yourself.

2. Loss of a family member or close friend may lead to feelings of depression. For example, your parents get a divorce, you move away from home for the first time and as a result are away from your friends and family, or you break up with your boyfriend/girlfriend.

3. Dwelling unnecessarily on negative events, such as failures and disappointment, instead of using the event as a learning experience. For example, perhaps you had a job interview, but you didn't get the job. Instead of getting depressed about it, think about what you learned from it and what you might do differently next time.

4. Judging or criticizing yourself and your abilities too harshly. For example, you criticize and blame yourself for your failures and disappointment.

5. Evaluating the outcome of situations as worse than they really are. For example, your supervisor asks you to make 15 copies of something, but you made 50. You're sure he's going to penalize you in some way.

6. Experiencing too much pressure from your parents and/or peers to meet the demands and expectations that they set out for you. Such pressure deprives you of the opportunity to develop your own identity and independence.

7. Setting unrealistic goals. For example, you just bought a computer and you want to learn a program by tomorrow. You need a realistic amount of time to learn a new skill.

8. Fear of failure. For example, if you get an "F" on an exam you may see yourself as a failure rather than as a perfectly worthwhile person who has failed an exam.

How to increase your self-confidence

1. Think positively about yourself.

2. Set goals that are realistic and that will allow you to meet your expectations. That is, set your goals at a reasonable level, so that what you accomplish is equal or almost equal to what you set out to accomplish. This can boost your self-confidence and self-satisfaction.

3. Reward/praise yourself when you have done well.

4. Whenever something upsetting or disappointing occurs, be aware of your thoughts. Try to think logically about the situation instead of reacting merely on the basis of your emotions.

5. Dwell on your strengths, not your weaknesses.

6. Realize that there are certain things that you are more adept and competent in than others, and that it is impossible to expect perfection in every aspect of your life.

7. Do not attribute your achievement and accomplishments only to luck. Instead, give yourself credit for your own personal achievement.

8. Learn to be assertive. That is, learn to express your feelings, opinions, beliefs, and needs directly, openly, and honestly, while not violating the rights of others. For example, learn to say "no" to unreasonable requests.

9. Make a list of what you feel are the major problems in your life. Then list ways to improve or change them. Chances are that not all of your problems can be dealt with easily or quickly. However, there are some areas where you can take immediate action.

Checklist for improving self-confidence

✓ Count the good things, not the negative ones.

✓ Think positively about yourself.

✓ Learn from your experiences.

✓ Set realistic goals.

✓ Be courageous.

✓ Keep learning.

✓ Live usefully.

✓ Welcome change.

Source: Counseling Center, Division of Student Affairs, State University of New York at Buffalo

Agreeing and disagreeing

When you are having a conversation with someone, you may or may not agree with what the person is saying. Use these common expressions to show that you agree or disagree about something.

To express agreement:

> I agree with you.
> That's what I was thinking.
> I know what you mean.
> I feel the same way.
> I think so, too.

To express disagreement:

> I don't agree.
> I don't know about that.
> I'm not sure I agree with you on that.
> I don't think so.
> I wouldn't say that.
> I don't mean to disagree with you but . . .

Say it! Use these expressions as you work with your classmate to figure out how the people in Exercise B lost or increased their self-confidence.

B. Interpret the article. Work with your classmates to interpret each section of the article.

STUDENTS 1 AND 2: **How does a lack of self-confidence develop?** Take turns reading the eight reasons why people lose their self-confidence. Fill in the blank with the number (or numbers) of the correct reason(s) next to each example.

__2__ 1. Mary has been dating Bill for several months. Suddenly he stops calling her.

_____ 2. Terry didn't pass the TOEFL test even though she studied very hard. She feels really dumb.

_____ 3. Your boss yelled at you at work because you accidentally burned the hamburger buns. You just know you're going to get fired.

_____ 4. John had a job interview but he didn't get the job. He can't stop thinking about how bad the interview was.

_____ 5. Your father always wanted you to be a doctor but you knew you weren't interested in medicine. You knew you were going to disappoint him.

_____ 6. Your best friend wants you to go to college with her but you really want to go to a vocational school to learn about computers.

_____ 7. You want to be a lawyer in three years, but you haven't passed the entrance test yet.

_____ 8. You didn't get the job at the department store. You're sure it's because your English isn't completely fluent.

STUDENTS 3 AND 4: **How to increase your self-confidence.** Take turns reading aloud the actions people can take to increase their self-confidence. Fill in the blank with the number (or numbers) of the action(s) that the person in the example took to do this.

___5___ 1. Mary realizes that her English isn't perfect, but she knows she has a nice smile and is friendly.

_____ 2. Tom writes down his problems and tries to come up with ways to solve them.

_____ 3. You go out to dinner with friends when you have done something well.

_____ 4. Jerry passed the TOEFL test. He knew he passed because he studied very hard for many months.

_____ 5. Ana wants to become a licensed vocational nurse, but she knows she should go step by step and take the certified nursing class first.

_____ 6. Your boss asked you to work in the mornings even though he knows you are taking classes. You had the courage to tell him that you couldn't do it.

_____ 7. Your boss would like you to take care of the customers, but she also counts on you to organize the merchandise quickly. You can't do everything and you know that. You point out that a coworker is very good at talking to customers.

_____ 8. You wanted to cry because your supervisor yelled at you. You stopped yourself and tried to understand the problem.

C. Teach each other. Share the information you learned in your section with each other.

STUDENT 1: Teach Student 3. Then switch roles.

STUDENT 2: Teach Student 4. Then switch roles.

EVALUATION: **Monitor and correct your work**

1. What did you learn about building self-confidence? Take a few minutes with your teammates to compare the ideas your team had about increasing self-confidence before you read the suggestions in the article.

2. Your teacher will read aloud a few examples from the exercises for each section of your article. Do you agree with the answers? Are other answers possible? Use the expressions you learned to express agreement or disagreement with your teacher.

 O N L I N E !

A. Search. For more information about self-esteem and self-confidence as they relate to career choice, look on the Internet. Look up these addresses or search on your own:

- Speaking of careers:
  http://www.acinet.org/resource/
  Click: Think about guidance and counseling

- Self-esteem personality test:
  http://www.queendom.com/selfest.html

B. Report. After you find the addresses, tell your classmates or write a brief paragraph about ways to overcome shyness.

N O T E

If you don't have a computer or cannot get on the Internet at home, you can:

1. Go to a public library near your home or school. Libraries usually have free Internet access.

2. Find out if you can get on the Internet at your school. Schools often have Internet access.

3. Ask a friend if you can use his or her computer to get on the Internet.

 Write it up!

PREPARATION: **Defining personal strengths**

As you read in the article, one way to increase your self-confidence is to dwell on your strengths.

■ Read the personal strength word list. Put a checkmark next to the words you know. Put a question mark next to the ones you don't know.

■ Work with one or two classmates to figure out the meaning of each word. Write a synonym or definition next to the words that are new for you. If necessary, use a dictionary.

Personal strength words

____	adaptable	____	knowledgeable
____	ambitious	____	loyal
____	analytical	____	meticulous
____	assertive	____	motivated
____	attentive	____	organized
____	capable	____	outgoing
____	cheerful	____	people-oriented
____	competent	____	perceptive
____	conscientious	____	personable
____	cooperative	____	polite
____	dedicated	____	productive
____	dependable	____	professional
____	detail-oriented	____	reliable
____	determined	____	resourceful
____	diplomatic	____	responsible
____	efficient	____	results-oriented
____	energetic	____	self-motivated
____	enthusiastic	____	self-starter
____	flexible	____	stable
____	forthright	____	task-oriented
____	goal-oriented	____	a team player
____	hardworking	____	a troubleshooter
____	high-achieving	____	trustworthy
____	innovative	____	versatile

A. Find the right personal strength word. Take turns reading the following descriptions with a partner. Find the personal strength word on the list that best applies to each description and use it.

EXAMPLE: When a computer or other equipment doesn't work immediately, I try to figure out what the problem is.

I'm a troubleshooter. OR I like to troubleshoot when there's a
problem with the equipment.

1. I'm happy when my duties change at work. I like to do many jobs at the same time.

   _____

2. My letters are always correct because I check them carefully.

   _____

3. I like to work as part of a team, and I like to help people.

   _____

4. In my last job, I was an inventory clerk. I made a list of what I needed to do every day. My desk was neat so I could always find the forms I needed.

   _____

5. I always come to work on time, and I always stay until the job is done. When I say I will do something, I do it.

   _____

B. Describe your own strengths. Look again at the list of personal strength words. Choose two of your best strengths from the list and write them down. Write your own specific examples of each strength based on an experience you had.

EXAMPLE: Strength: I'm enthusiastic.
At my last job as busboy, even though I didn't earn much money, I
was always in a good mood and did my job well. I was friendly to the
customers and made them feel comfortable.

1. Strength #1: _____

   _____

   _____

2. Strength #2: _____

   _____

   _____

EVALUATION: **Monitor and correct your work**

After you finish writing, give your description of your strengths to a classmate. Your classmate will evaluate your description by completing this revision checklist.

Classmate Revision Checklist

WRITER'S NAME: _____

CHECKER'S NAME: _____

Circle *yes* or *no*.

1. Can you read the writer's handwriting?   YES   NO
   (If you circled *no*, ask the writer to rewrite it.)

2. Does everything you read make sense?   YES   NO
   (If you circled *no*, ask the writer to explain what you
   didn't understand and help him/her correct it.)

3. Are all the verbs in the correct tense?   YES   NO
   (If you circled *no*, help the writer correct them.)

4. Are all the words spelled correctly?   YES   NO
   (If you're not sure of the spelling, use a dictionary.)

5. Does every sentence begin with a capital letter?   YES   NO

6. Does every sentence end with a period?   YES   NO

7. Do you have the same strengths as your classmate?   YES   NO

Think about the job you have now or a job you would like to have in the future. Look at the personal strength word list.

The job I want to get in the future is _____.

Rank the most important strengths for that job from 1 to 10, with 1 being the most important and 10 the least important for your career field.

1. _____
2. _____
3. _____
4. _____
5. _____
6. _____
7. _____
8. _____
9. _____
10. _____

Write a paragraph explaining why you chose the first two strengths as the most important ones for your particular job.

_____

_____

_____

_____

_____

_____

_____

_____

Role-play the following situation with a group of three students.

ROLES: Director, assistant manager, and personnel director of a company.

TASK: The company has grown and you must hire several new employees.

SITUATION: At a meeting you discuss:
(1) the **qualifications** that the new employees should have. What kind of people do you want to hire, and why?
(2) the **incentives** your company will offer to attract new employees.

HOW TO COMPLETE THE TASK:
Use the chart to organize the qualifications and incentives for each job. Fill out the chart together.

Employee Qualifications and Incentives

Name of the company _____

Names of the director, assistant manager, and personnel director _____

_____

Type of company _____

List three jobs in your company and the qualifications for each one. Then describe the incentives your company will offer to attract good applicants to work at your company.

You are looking for people to fill three jobs at your company. For each job, list the two or three most important qualifications. Then write a paragraph describing the kind of person you are seeking and why.	Write down two incentives you are offering to attract these new employees. Then write a paragraph describing these incentives and explaining why they are better than the ones your competitors are offering.

Job #1:	Job #2:	Job #3:	Incentive #1:	Incentive #2:

◆ Practical grammar: Spelling

Look at these phrases from the dictation. In the spaces below, rewrite the base form of each word in bold type. The base form of a verb is the verb without the **-ing** ending.

setting realistic goals   _____

studying   _____

welcoming change   _____

Notice that the base form of the first word is **set** but its **-ing** form is **setting** with a double **t**. There are certain spelling rules to help you remember how to spell commonly used words. See if you can figure out a few of these spelling rules. If you figure out the rules yourself, you might remember them later.

Can you do it? Look at the words in column A. Pay special attention to the words that have the consonant-vowel-consonant (C-V-C) pattern. Then look at the same words with **-ing** endings in column B. What happens to the final consonant in the words that have a consonant-vowel-consonant pattern?

A	B	
rub	rubbing	
dig	digging	
run	running	C-V-C words
shop	shopping	
_____	_____	
earn	earning	
lend	lending	
meet	meeting	non C-V-C words
eat	eating	
_____	_____	

1. Write the spelling rule.

_____

2. Add two more words that fit the pattern to each list above.

Can you do it? Look at the words in column A. Then look at the same words with **-ing** and **-ed** endings in columns B and C. Do you see a pattern?

A	B	C
study	studying	studied
bury	burying	buried
try	trying	tried
stay	staying	stayed
pray	praying	prayed
_____	_____	_____

1. Write the spelling rule.

_____

2. Add one more word that fits the pattern to the list above.

Summary of spelling rules:

1. Verbs that end with the consonant-vowel-consonant pattern

    a. If the verb has one syllable and ends with the consonant-vowel-consonant pattern, double the final consonant.

set	setting
plan	planning

       EXCEPTIONS: **w** and **x** are not doubled.

fix	fixing
grow	growing

    b. If a verb ending with the consonant-vowel-consonant pattern has two syllables and the first syllable is stressed, do not double the final consonant.

listen	listening
open	opening

    c. If the verb has two syllables and the second syllable is stressed, double the consonant.

begin	beginning
refer	referring

2. Verbs that end in **-y**

    a. If **-y** is preceded by a consonant, keep the **-y** and add **-ing**. If **-y** is preceded by a consonant, change **-y** to **-i** and add **-ed**.

study	studying
study	studied
try	trying
try	tried

    b. If **-y** is preceded by a vowel, keep the **-y**.

stay	staying
stay	stayed

3. Verbs that end in **-e**

If the verb ends in **-e**, drop the **-e** and add **-ing**. If the verb ends in **-e**, just add **-d**.

welcome	welcoming
welcome	welcomed

EXCEPTIONS: If a verb ends in **-ee**, the final **-e** is not dropped.

agree	agreeing

PRACTICE

A. Some new hires. The director of a company sent an e-mail to all the managers. Fill in each blank with the correct word from the bank of words below. Spell the words according to the spelling rules you learned.

plan	write	open
set	hire	try

```
I'm _____ (1) every department leader to get input
on the _____ (2) process. We are _____ (3) to
write the classified ad for three new assemblers. I'm
_____ (4) up this process to everyone. Please e-
mail the qualities you'd like to see in your coworkers.
Here in management we are _____ (5) to involve
everyone in the employment process. We're _____
(6) up the interviews for next month, so send me your
responses ASAP.
```

B. Qualifications. The managers answered the director's request by e-mail. Fill in each blank with the correct word from the bank of words below. Spell the words according to the spelling rules you learned.

plan	reply	hope
study	begin	hire

We are _____ (1) to your e-mail for input on the assemblers you are _____ (2) to hire. We are _____ (3) to assemble new cellular phones. Therefore, the other managers and I are _____ (4) that you'll hire assemblers who have _____ (5) the latest soldering techniques. We believe that _____ (6) assemblers who do not know these new techniques would take a lot of time out of our schedules. We are willing to do it if necessary, but if at all possible, we request that the new employees already know the procedures.

 # Check it!

Put a checkmark next to each activity you accomplished in this chapter.

ACADEMIC SKILLS CHECKLIST

Did you . . .

_____ write new vocabulary words in a notebook?

_____ write new grammar rules in a notebook?

_____ describe some of your personal strengths?

_____ interpret and communicate information from the article?

_____ use resources in the classroom, such as a dictionary or a thesaurus?

_____ revise a classmate's paragraph using the revision checklist?

_____ spell common words correctly using the rules you learned?

_____ use the Internet to get more information about the topic?

WORK SKILLS CHECKLIST

Did you . . .

_____ work well with your group members?

_____ teach others the information you learned? What is one thing you taught? _____

_____

_____ rank your strengths from the most to the least important?

_____ cooperate and give ideas during the role play?

_____ think creatively when you filled out the chart?

_____ use expressions to agree or disagree with someone? What is one expression you used? _____

_____

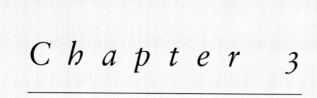

Chapter 3

Volunteering: On-the-Job Training

By the end of this chapter, you will be able to:

- Teach classmates information you acquired from an article.

- Identify places where you might volunteer.

- Give examples of how volunteering might help you find work later.

- Write a summary of an article using a chart.

- Revise and edit your own and a classmate's summary.

- Make questions and give answers using the present perfect tense.

- Use appropriate language to express your opinions.

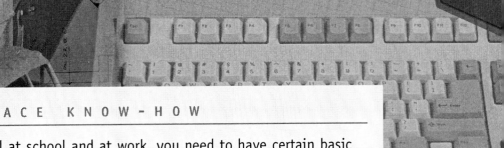

To be successful at school and at work, you need to have certain basic skills and qualities. In this chapter, you will focus on the following skills and qualities:

1. Making predictions

2. Working in teams

3. Organizing information on a chart

4. Monitoring and correcting pronunciation

Talk about it!

1. Have you ever worked as a volunteer? Where? What did you do?

2. If you have volunteered, was it a worthwhile experience? Why or why not?

Take it down!

Your teacher will dictate a paragraph that covers the content and the grammar in this chapter. First write what you hear. Then check it by using the Dictation Revision Form on the back inside cover.

_____

_____

_____

_____

_____

 Read about it!

PREPARATION: **Thinking about volunteering**

In a group of four students, look at the ads for volunteers and discuss these questions.

1. Do any of these ads appeal to you? Which ones? Why?

2. What benefits do you think there might be in doing volunteer work? Make a list.

♥ **HEALTH** ♥

AGENCY: Denver Hospice
NEED: Errands, companionship, clerical support
SITE: Downtown area
MINIMUM TIME: 3 hrs. per week after 20 hours training course
CONTACT: Judy Davidson, 555-2344

LITERACY

AGENCY: Dallas Committee on Literacy
NEED: Tutors to teach basic reading, writing, and math skills to children
SITE: Throughout the city
MINIMUM TIME: Three hours per week; three month commitment, plus training
CONTACT: 555-0933

Animals

AGENCY: Make People Smile Animal Therapy
NEED: Volunteers and their pets to visit hospitals & nursing homes
SITE: Throughout county
MINIMUM TIME: Four hours per month.
CONTACT: Mike, 555-6000

HUMAN SERVICES

AGENCY: Mat's Thrift Store
NEED: Part-time administrative assistant to help Mat: office, computer skills needed.
SITE: Near airport
MINIMUM TIME: Four to 12 hours per week, March through June.
CONTACT: Mat, 555-4478

Expressing opinions

There are many occasions when you will want to express your opinion, or when someone will ask you for it: in meetings or conversations with your supervisor or coworkers, in class discussions and study groups. Use these common expressions when you are giving your opinion about something:

I think that . . .
In my opinion . . .
It seems to me that . . .
As I see it . . .
Not everyone will agree with me, but . . .
You know what I think? I think that . . .

Say It! Use these expressions to express your opinion as you discuss the benefits of volunteering with your classmates.

PRACTICE: **Guessing from context**

A. Read the article. In your group of four students, silently read the article up to the section **Apprenticeships.** Try not to use your dictionary the first time you read. By reading the sentence that contains a new word and the sentences before and after it, you should be able to guess the meaning of any words you do not understand.

On-the-Job Training

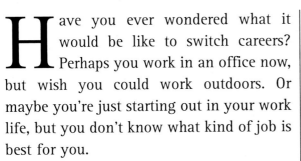

Have you ever wondered what it would be like to switch careers? Perhaps you work in an office now, but wish you could work outdoors. Or maybe you're just starting out in your work life, but you don't know what kind of job is best for you.

One of the best ways to experiment with work is to "try it on" by doing it part-time, or on a short-term basis. And one of the best ways to do that is through volunteer work.

Many people have volunteered in the past, usually for reasons of charity or good will. If you're a frequent volunteer, you're already aware of the emotional benefits you gain from helping someone else.

But volunteering as a career-development tool is often overlooked. That's too bad, because volunteering is an excellent path toward sharpened skills, strong networking contacts, and a higher awareness of one or several fields.

The range of volunteer possibilities is nearly endless. Career-explorers have volunteered as carpenters, bricklayers, accountants, tax preparers, teachers, writers, designers, caretakers, coaches – even as heads of nonprofit organizations.

In almost all the cases, the volunteers would not have had the credentials required to be hired for pay; nevertheless, under supervision, their aptitudes and willingness to learn allowed them to develop their skills. In many cases, the workers later switched fields successfully.

Flexible assignments

A primary advantage of using volunteer assignments to explore careers is the short commitment required. Unlike formal training programs, the volunteer usually can sign on for a specific project and leave when it is completed. Volunteer assignments usually are flexible, allowing the workers to maintain their regular jobs or school programs; they also allow the workers more responsibility more quickly than most work-for-pay situations would provide.

To find an appropriate volunteer situation, check the Yellow Pages under Social Service Organizations for a local volunteer center. Or call your United Way office and ask about volunteer "clearing houses" in your community.

Don't forget about nonprofit board management. If you're trying to develop leadership or management skills, you might enjoy being a board member for a nonprofit organization in which you believe. However you find your volunteer assignment, you'll want to follow these steps to ensure the work pays off in career growth:

- ◆ Define the skills you want to sharpen or the kinds of people you want to serve. When you meet with a potential supervisor in a volunteer assignment, discuss those goals.

- ◆ Ask about training programs and the level of responsibility you might have. If the situation seems right, sign on and have fun!

- ◆ At the end of the assignment, collect letters of recommendation or create a summary report of your progress to help communicate your new level of ability to a future employer.

While volunteer assignments will provide enough training to allow you at least entry-level access to some careers, other fields will not open their doors so easily. For example, the building, printing, and machine trades are all industries that reserve their best jobs for workers with the best training. Working as an apprentice is a very good way to get that training.

Apprenticeships

The roots of apprenticeship training are at least 500 years old. Indeed, Benjamin Franklin was an apprentice printer, indentured to work for his employer/trainer for seven or eight years before he was released to work on his own.

Modern apprenticeships last from one to six years and include a mixture of classroom training and hands-on work. They are established by companies or unions and follow a specified course of progress.

Usually, the worker is paid about half of the wages of a fully trained worker for the first year or more of the program. Wage increases of 10 percent occur over the next two or more years, followed by "graduation" to full journeyman wages and responsibilities. The final step in the process is to become a master craftsman, indicating you have become an expert in your field.

More than 230,000 Americans currently are registered in the United States as apprentices in more than 700 crafts. New fields are added each year, and a few are dropped as the economy changes.

To explore apprenticeship opportunities, ask for information from the Bureau of Apprenticeship Training in your state or at the federal level. Then tour the companies where you might apprentice and talk with the employers to compare your goals and expectations.

Because of an increased need for skilled workers in the trades, this is an excellent time to consider an apprenticeship program.

"On-the-job training" by Amy Lindgren, Knight-Ridder/Tribune Information Services. The article was reprinted in the *San Diego Union-Tribune*, 2/24/97.

B. Work together. In a group of four students, give each student a number from 1-4.

STUDENTS 1 AND 2: Work together on items 1–4 on the next page.

STUDENTS 3 AND 4: Work together on items 5–8 on the next page.

With your partner, write synonyms (words with similar meanings) for the words in your sentences. Then rewrite each sentence with your new word.

EXAMPLE: Volunteering is an excellent path toward sharpened skills, *strong networking contacts,* and a higher awareness of one or several fields.

synonym for *strong networking contacts*: meeting people in a related field

sentence with new word: Volunteering is an excellent path toward sharpened skills, meeting people in a related field, and a higher awareness of one or several fields.

When you have finished, look up each word in the dictionary to see if you are correct. If you need additional clues, use the bank of synonyms below.

unlimited	forgotten	guarantee
obligation	readiness	change
professions	generosity	

1. Have you ever wondered what it would be like to *switch* careers?

   synonym for *switch*: _____

   sentence with your new word: _____

   _____

   _____

2. Many people have volunteered in the past, usually for reasons of *charity* or *good will.*

   synonym for *charity* or *good will:* _____

   sentence with your new word: _____

   _____

   _____

3. But volunteering as a career development tool is often *overlooked.*

   synonym for *overlooked*: _____

   sentence with your new word: _____

   _____

   _____

4. The range of volunteer possibilities is nearly *endless.*

   synonym for *endless*: _____

   sentence with your new word: _____

   _____

   _____

5. Under supervision, their aptitudes and *willingness* to learn allowed them to develop their skills.

   synonym for *willingness*: _____

   sentence with your new word: _____

   _____

6. In many cases, the workers later switched *fields* successfully.

synonym for *fields*: _____

sentence with your new word: _____

_____

_____

7. A primary advantage of using volunteer assignments to explore careers is the short *commitment* required.

synonym for *commitment*: _____

sentence with new word: _____

_____

_____

8. You'll want to follow these steps to *ensure* the work pays off in career growth.

synonym for *ensure*: _____

sentence with your synonym: _____

_____

_____

C. Teach each other. Share the new vocabulary words you learned with each other.

STUDENT 1: Explain your words to Student 3. Then switch roles.

STUDENT 2: Explain your words to Student 4. Then switch roles.

D. True or false? Your teacher will give you a short quiz to see if you understood each other.

1.   T   F

2.   T   F

3.   T   F

4.   T   F

5.   T   F

A. Think about it. In your groups of four, answer the following questions.

STUDENTS 1 AND 2: Answer questions 1–3.

STUDENTS 3 AND 4: Answer questions 4–5.

ALL STUDENTS: Answer question 6.

1. Look at the list of benefits of volunteering that you wrote before you read the article. How do your reasons compare with the ones in the article? _____

_____

_____

_____

_____

2. Is it possible to have a regular job and volunteer at the same time? Explain. _____

_____

_____

_____

_____

3. What is the United Way? What is a volunteer clearinghouse?

_____

_____

_____

_____

4. The article discusses four reasons why people volunteer. Describe these reasons in your own words. _____

_____

_____

_____

5. A friend of yours has moved here from another city. Although he has work experience, he wants to volunteer. Why? _____

_____

_____

_____

6. What would be one of the greatest benefits of volunteering for you?

_____

_____

_____

B. Teach each other. Explain your answers to your teammate.

STUDENT 1: Explain your answers to Student 3. Then switch roles.

STUDENT 2: Explain your answers to Student 4. Then switch roles.

EVALUATION: **Monitor and correct your work**

Your teacher will assign students to write their answers on the board.

 ONLINE!

A. **Search.** For more information about volunteering, look on the Internet. You can either try this address or search on your own:

■ http://www.unitedway-cal.org

B. **Report.** After you find the address, tell your classmates or write a brief paragraph about different places to volunteer in your area.

NOTE

If you don't have a computer or cannot get on the Internet at home, you can:

1. Go to a public library near your home or school. Libraries usually have free Internet access.

2. Find out if you can get on the Internet at your school. Schools often have Internet access.

3. Ask a friend if you can use his or her computer to get on the Internet.

Write it up!

Clustering is a strategy that will help you organize your thoughts so that you can write in a clear and organized manner. It is especially useful for writing a report or a summary of important information, something you may frequently have to do at school or at work. Follow these steps to prepare a cluster chart of information for a summary of the article you read.

Form a group of three students. Work together to fill out the chart below. Include as many examples as possible in each cluster. Refer back to the article if you need to.

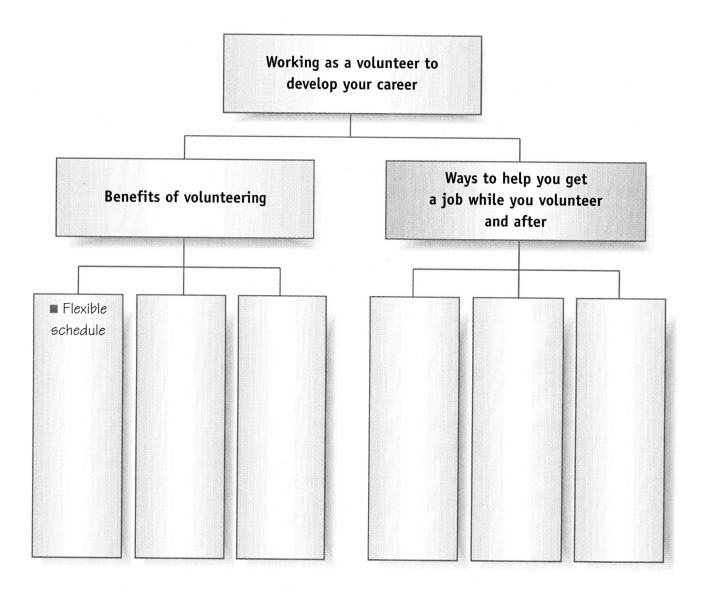

Working as a volunteer to develop your career

Benefits of volunteering

Ways to help you get a job while you volunteer and after

■ Flexible schedule

Writing a summary

Write a summary of the article using your clusters. You may do this with another student or alone. Be sure to include: (1) three benefits of volunteering, (2) three ways to help you get a job while you are volunteering and after you finish volunteering.

E V A L U A T I O N : **Monitor and correct your work**

When you have finished writing your summary, find a partner and read it aloud to him or her. Remember these basic pronunciation rules as you listen to your teacher read some examples from the article:

■ **Speak slowly.**

   Perhaps you work in an office now, but wish you could work outdoors.

■ **Emphasize the stressed syllables of the words.**

   A primary advantage of using volunteer assignments to explore careers is the short commitment required.

■ **Your voice should go down at the end of a sentence.**

   The range of volunteer possibilities is nearly endless.

H O W   T O   S A Y   I T

Asking for repetition or clarification

When listening to a supervisor, a coworker, a teacher, or a classmate, you may not always hear or understand everything that person is saying. You may use the following expressions to ask someone to repeat or clarify what he or she said:

   I didn't hear you.
   I didn't catch that.
   I missed that part.
   Could you repeat the last thing you said?
   Would you mind saying that again?
   Sorry, I don't see what you mean.

Say it! Use these expressions to ask your classmates for clarification as you read your summaries to each other.

After you read your summary aloud, give it to your classmate to check. Your classmate will evaluate the summary by completing this revision checklist.

Classmate Revision Checklist

WRITER'S NAME: _____

CHECKER'S NAME: _____

Circle *yes* or *no*.

1. Can you read the writer's handwriting?   YES   NO
   (If you circled *no*, ask the writer to rewrite it.)

2. Did the writer give three benefits of volunteering?   YES   NO

3. Did the writer give three ways to help get a   YES   NO
   job volunteering?

4. Are the verbs in the correct tense?   YES   NO
   (If you circled *no*, help the writer correct them.)

5. Are all the words spelled correctly?   YES   NO
   (If you circled *no*, help the writer make
   corrections. If you're not sure of the spelling,
   use a dictionary.)

6. Does every sentence begin with a capital letter?   YES   NO

7. Does every sentence end with a period?   YES   NO

◆ Practical grammar: The present perfect vs. the past tense

In the third paragraph of the article, you read this sentence:

> Many people **have volunteered** in the past, usually for reasons of charity or good will.

The tense of that sentence is the present perfect.

USAGE

Use the present perfect tense for these situations:

RULE 1: If an action is completed but you don't know exactly when it finished:

> Many people **have volunteered** in the past.
> (You don't know exactly when the people volunteered.)

> The clerk **has** already **given** the customer his change.
> (The clerk gave the customer his change but you don't know exactly when.)

NOTE

When giving an exact or approximate time, use the past tense instead of the present perfect:

> Mary **volunteered** at a hospital last year.
> (You know when she volunteered.)

> The clerk gave the customer his money a few minutes ago.
> (The clerk gave the customer his change and you know when it happened.)

The word **ago** is not used with the present perfect tense.

RULE 2: If an action occurred repeatedly in the past and you think it might occur again:

> The doctor **has seen** several patients so far this morning.
> (The doctor has seen several patients today and she might see some more.)

RULE 3: If an action started in the past and is continuing in the present:

The woman **has worked** for ten years.

Certain words trigger the present perfect. When you hear or read these words, it is a signal that the present perfect tense will probably follow:

ever	several times
never	for
yet	since
already	so far

FORM

Form the present perfect by using the helping verb (sometimes called the auxiliary verb) **have** or **has** and the past participle of the verb:

Many people **have volunteered** in the past
AUXILIARY + VERB PAST PARTICIPLE

The past participles of regular verbs look just like regular verbs in the past tense: both end in **-ed.**

Can you do it? With a partner, read the sentences below. Underline the helping verbs. Circle the past participles or verbs in the past tense. Write the tense of each sentence and explain why it is in that tense by citing the appropriate rule (1, 2, or 3) from the section above.

TENSE   RULE

1. _____   ____   Tony volunteered to work overtime on Friday.

2. _____   ____   Tony has volunteered to work overtime several times this month.

3. _____   ____   The students studied for the test yesterday.

4. _____   ____   The students have studied for the test for one hour.

5. _____   ____   Sara typed the letter for her friend last night.

6. _____   ____   Sara has already typed the letter for her friend.

The past participles of irregular verbs must be memorized. You probably already know many of these verbs because you use them often.

Can you do it? With a partner, underline the helping verbs. Circle the irregular verbs. Talk about why the present perfect tense is used.

1. _____ She has been in the United States for five years.

2. _____ The supervisor has already sent the managers an e-mail.

3. _____ The teacher hasn't seen the movie yet.

4. _____ The students have already taken the TOEFL test.

5. _____ The graduate student has written three reports so far.

PRACTICE

A. Analyze the verbs. With a partner, examine the verbs in Exercise B and decide if each one is regular or irregular. If you aren't sure, look at the irregular verb list on page 183. If the verb is regular, underline it. If the verb is irregular, circle it.

B. Have you ever . . . ? Walk around the room and ask questions in the present perfect tense to find out who has done the following tasks. When you find someone who answers yes, he or she must:

■ Answer the question completely, using either the past or present perfect tense.

■ Give you his/her name and spell it so that you can write it in the correct column. Each person can answer only two questions from the same sheet.

EXAMPLE: Use a Macintosh computer.

STUDENT A: Have you ever used a Macintosh computer?

STUDENT B: Yes, I've used a Macintosh many times.
In fact, I used one yesterday in class.

STUDENT A: Please spell your name.

STUDENT B: Thong. T-H-O-N-G.

STUDENT A: Thank you.

Have you ever . . . ?   (STUDENT'S NAME)

1. take dictation at the blackboard?   _____

2. have a job in this city? (what job?)   _____

3. fall asleep during a meeting?   _____

4. feel proud of something?   _____

5. eat out with a classmate or coworker?   _____
   (at what restaurant?)

6. serve customers in a restaurant?   _____

7. do volunteer work? (where?)   _____

8. speak English in front of several people? _____

9. find information on the Internet?   _____
   (what information?)

10. teach a classmate something?   _____

11. give an injection to someone? (to whom?) _____

12. write a business letter? (what kind?)   _____

13. translate for someone?   _____

14. send an e-mail? (to whom?)   _____

15. use a computer? (what kind?)   _____

C. What have your classmates done? Write at least five sentences about what you have learned about your classmates. Use their names and the present perfect tense.

_____

_____

_____

_____

_____

_____

After you write your sentences, give them to a classmate to read. Your classmate will check them by completing this revision checklist.

Classmate Revision Checklist

WRITER'S NAME: _____

CHECKER'S NAME: _____

Circle *yes* or *no*.

1. Can you read the writer's handwriting?   YES   NO
   (If you circled *no*, ask the writer to rewrite it.)

2. Are there at least five sentences?   YES   NO

3. Did you understand all the sentences?   YES   NO
   (If you answered *no*, ask the writer to
   explain what wasn't clear and help him
   or her to clarify it.)

4. Are all the verbs used correctly?   YES   NO
   (If you circled *no*, help correct them.)

5. Are all the words spelled correctly?   YES   NO
   (If you circled *no*, help the writer make corrections.
   If you're not sure of the spelling, use a dictionary.)

6. Does every sentence begin with a capital letter?   YES   NO

7. Does every sentence end with a period?   YES   NO

 # Check it!

Put a checkmark next to each activity you accomplished in this chapter.

ACADEMIC SKILLS CHECKLIST

Did you . . .

_____ write new vocabulary words in a notebook?

_____ write new grammar rules in a notebook?

_____ anticipate the reading topic by thinking of some benefits of volunteering before you read the article?

_____ guess the meaning of new vocabulary words from the context (that is, from the surrounding sentences)?

_____ use a chart to write a summary of the article you read?

_____ write, revise, and edit a summary?

_____ follow the pronunciation rules when you read your summary aloud?

_____ make suggestions about your partner's pronunciation? Which pronunciation suggestions did you make? _____

_____ ask questions and give answers correctly in the present perfect tense?

_____ use the correct verb form in the present perfect tense?

_____ learn some new things about your classmates?

_____ use the Internet to get more information about the topic?

WORK SKILLS CHECKLIST

Did you . . .

_____ work effectively in a team or group with students from diverse backgrounds?

_____ teach something new to a classmate? What did you teach?

_____

_____ make decisions about which verbs to use?

_____ organize your ideas in a cluster?

_____ use a computer to type your summary?

_____ use appropriate language to express your opinion? What is one expression you used? _____

_____

_____ use appropriate language to ask for repetition or clarification? What is one expression you used? _____

_____

_____ use resources in the classroom, such as a dictionary or thesaurus?

C h a p t e r 4

Effective Job Applications

By the end of this chapter, you will be able to:

- Teach classmates information you acquired from an article.

- Demonstrate your ability to work effectively in teams to complete certain tasks.

- Identify steps to take before filling out a job application.

- Demonstrate your ability to fill out an application completely and accurately.

- Revise and edit your own and a classmate's application.

- Write a paragraph to complement a job application.

- Apply the rules for using capitalization, punctuation, and the past tense in application forms.

- Use appropriate language to give suggestions.

To be successful at school and at work, you need to have certain basic skills and qualities. In this chapter you will focus on the following skills and qualities:

1. Using clues to make predictions

2. Monitoring and correcting pronunciation for questions

3. Interpreting and communicating information from an article

4. Organizing information on a job application

5. Writing a descriptive paragraph for a job application

Talk about it!

1. Have you ever filled out a job application? What information do you need to fill out a job application completely?

2. Are all job applications the same? What are some similarities and differences in job applications?

Take it down!

Your teacher will dictate a paragraph that covers the content and the grammar in this chapter. First, write what you hear. Then check it by using the Dictation Revision Form on the back inside cover.

_____

_____

_____

_____

_____

◆ Read about it!

PREPARATION: **Making predictions**

Being able to make predictions about the content of an article or other text will make you a better reader. The title and section titles of the article usually contain important clues about the topic. Using what you already know about the topic, as well as your common sense, will also help you make accurate predictions about the article.

In a group of three students, number 1–3. This is your home group. Work together to predict what the article is about by answering the questions. Each person in the group will take one of the following jobs:

LEADER (#1 STUDENTS): Be sure everyone in your group gives his or her opinion to each question. There is no right or wrong answer.

RECORDER AND REPORTER (#2 STUDENTS): Take notes on your group's answers. Don't worry about spelling and grammar. You will report your group's answers to the whole class.

READER (#3 STUDENTS): Read each question to your group. Follow these pronunciation rules:

- Speak slowly.
- Emphasize the stressed syllables of the words.
- Your voice should go down at the end of a sentence.

1. The title of the article you will read is "Neatness Counts." What do you think this article will be about? _____
   _____
   _____

2. What do you think the author says to do before you start filling out a job application? Why? _____
   _____
   _____

3. What should you write on a job application in response to the question, "What salary do you expect?" _____
   _____
   _____

4. Why do you think you shouldn't use a pencil on a job application?

_____

_____

5. Can you leave anything blank on a job application? _____

_____

_____

EVALUATION: **Monitor and correct your work**

Your teacher will ask each group reporter to tell the predictions of his or her group. After you read the article, you will see how good your predictions were.

PRACTICE: **Interpreting and communicating information**

A. Read the article. Split up as follows to read the article.

ALL #1 STUDENTS: Read the section **Fill out a job application completely** together.

ALL #2 STUDENTS: Read the section **Job applications vary** together.

ALL #3 STUDENTS: Read the sections **Good answers** and **Get prepared** together.

Sloppy or incomplete work in filling out a job application makes employers doubt our ability.

✔ **Fill out a job application completely**

The way you fill out a job application can tell the prospective employer as much as or more than your answers.

Partially completed applications or scribbled answers place doubts about potential job performance in the employer's mind, said Brenda Hunzeker, branch supervisor of Accountants On Call and Accountants Executive Search.

"If it (the application) is sloppy and unorganized, what does that tell you about their work?" she said. "There's nothing more frustrating than coming out to interview someone and seeing 'See résumé' all over their application instead of answers.

"You question whether those people can follow directions or not."

Many employers want a completed application for their files, even if job candidates submit a résumé, said Dave McEachern, administrative services manager for the Kansas Department of Human Resources.

"A lot of people attach a résumé and don't complete and sign the application," McEachern explained. "Some employers won't consider that."

✔ Job applications vary

Applications differ according to the company and, sometimes, the job. Some are in-depth, others require only basic information.

The very first thing you should do is to read the application thoroughly, employment experts advise. Otherwise, you might use cursive writing when it clearly stated that you are to print.

Follow directions and fill out the application completely and as honestly as possible. Print neatly or use a typewriter if you are allowed to fill out the application away from the office. Be sure there are no mark overs or changes, said Marsha Willis, president of Advanced Careers of Kansas City Inc.

If you include a résumé, don't refer to it instead of answering questions such as those dealing with educational background or previous work experience.

Unless the employer or application clearly states that questions must be answered in pencil, use a pen. Bring one with black or blue ink, not red or other colors, experts advise.

There are several reasons for using pen. Your answers can't easily be erased and changed by someone else. Pencil can be hard to read and doesn't copy well, a problem if several people need to see your application.

Employers are not supposed to ask some questions such as age, ethnic origin, religion, marital status, number of children and health restrictions that are not disabilities, Hunzeker said. Applicants may leave such questions blank.

✔ Good answers

Willis advises job seekers not to put in a dollar amount when asked about desired salary.

"That could work against you," she said. "If they think the amount you put is too low, they could wonder what's wrong with you that you're not worth more. If it's too high, you'll have to prove every step of the way that you are worth that salary. And that's a lot of work emotionally."

Instead, Willis advises putting the word "open" in that slot. While "negotiable" has a negative connotation, "'open' is a friendly thing," she said.

✓ Get prepared

Before getting an application, write down the names, addresses, and phone numbers of people you will use as references.

List the high schools, colleges, and trade schools you attended, along with the years you graduated.

Compile a complete list of previous employment, along with addresses, years of employment, supervisors' names and phone numbers, and your job duties in that position. Don't attach the list to the application: write the information in, employment agents said.

Once you have completed your application, read it again, carefully, before handing it in. Check punctuation, spelling and grammar.

If there are mistakes that can't be corrected neatly, ask for another application.

Be sure your final product presents an image of a neat, conscientious, and organized worker who follows directions.

Source: Paula Barr
Kansas City Star, 4/27/97

B. Interpret the article. Work with your classmates to interpret each section of the article by answering the questions below. Do not copy from the article. Instead, **paraphrase** the article, that is, explain what the article says in your own words.

#1 STUDENTS: **Fill out a job application completely**

1. What does a messy or incomplete application say about a job applicant? _____

   _____

   _____

   _____

2. What do some employers do if an applicant doesn't sign the application? _____

   _____

   _____

   _____

3. In this section, there are many words about filling out job applications that have negative connotations, or meanings.

   ■ Find the five words that have negative connotations and highlight them in the article.

   ■ Find a synonym or a similar word or expression for each word you highlighted. Use the word bank below. The first one is done for you.

messy	confusing
written with poor handwriting	disappointing
uncertainty	incomplete

   a. _Partially completed = Incomplete_

   b. _____

   c. _____

   d. _____

   e. _____

   f. _____

#2 STUDENTS: **Job applications vary**

1. Why should you read the entire application before you begin filling it out? _____

   _____

2. Why should you not use a pencil when you fill out an application?

   _____

   _____

   _____

3. Write four questions employers are not supposed to ask job applicants.

   _____

   _____

   _____

   _____

4. What can an applicant do if any of the questions in number #3 are on the application? _____

_____

5. Highlight these words in your section of the article and find synonyms for them in the word bank below.

completely   says
vary   full of details
if not   former

a. differ = _____

b. in-depth = _____

c. thoroughly = _____

d. otherwise = _____

e. previous = _____

f. states = _____

#3 STUDENTS: **Good answers** and **Get prepared**

1. What should a job applicant write when asked about salary?

_____

_____

_____

2. Before taking a job application, what should an applicant do? List at least three things.

_____

_____

_____

3. After filling out the job application, what should an applicant do?

_____

_____

_____

4. Highlight these words in your section of the article and find a synonym or a similar word or expression for each one from the word bank below.

responsibilities   vocational schools
person looking for a job   space
to ask yourself something   collect

a. job seeker = _____

b. wonder = _____

c. slot = _____

d. trade schools = _____

e. compile = _____

f. duties = _____

C. **Teach each other.** Return to your home group. Teach your classmates the information you learned in your section, and find out about the sections you did not prepare.

■ Listen carefully to your classmates as they speak. Ask questions so that you can write answers to the questions for the sections you did not prepare.

■ When you teach the vocabulary words in your section, show your classmates where the words are and explain the meanings carefully. When other teammates present the vocabulary in their sections, ask, "What does _____ mean?" and point out the word you highlighted.

D. **Comprehension check.** Circle **T** or **F** to indicate whether each statement is true or false.

1. T   F   It is acceptable to leave blanks on a job application.

2. T   F   In some cases, pencil is acceptable on a job application.

3. T   F   You must type a job application.

4. T   F   It is better to write "open" than "negotiable" for the salary you want.

5. T   F   It is acceptable for employers to ask, "Why did you quit your last job?"

Discuss your answers with your home group. If you do not agree on any of the answers, defend your answer.

Practical grammar: Capitalization, punctuation, and past tense on application forms

CAPITALIZATION

Capitalize the following words in job applications, résumés, and correspondence:

RULE 1:   the first word of a sentence

RULE 2:   proper nouns (names of people, cities, states)

RULE 3:   titles, when they are written before a name

RULE 4:   names of organizations and companies

RULE 5:   days of the week, months of the year, and holidays

RULE 6:   the first word in the greeting of a letter

RULE 7:   the first word in the closing of a letter

Can you do it? Rewrite the sentences below, capitalizing the words correctly. Then write the letter of the rule that gives the reason for capitalizing in each case.

EXAMPLE: I didn't know mrs. Johnson got a promotion.

<u>I didn't know Mrs. Johnson got a promotion.</u>   Rule: <u>3</u>

1. Ana did seasonal work during the christmas vacation.

   _____   Rule: ____

2. He started working there in february.

   _____   Rule: ____

3. the shipment arrived last wednesday.

   _____   Rule: ____

4. The employee relocated to dallas.

   _____   Rule: ____

5. She just got a job at the store called great ideas gifts.

   _____   Rule: ____

6. The shores hotel is looking for front desk clerks.

_____ Rule: ____

7. The firm has branches in oregon.

_____ Rule: ____

8. dear dr. Anderson,

_____ Rule: ____

9. thank you for your interest in our new medical product.

_____ Rule: ____

10. sincerely yours,

_____ Rule: ____

PUNCTUATION

Here are some rules for using punctuation in job applications, résumés, and correspondence:

period (.)

Use a period after most abbreviations:

Mr.	Ms.	Dr.
Ave.	Apt.	U.S.

EXCEPTIONS: IBM, UN, AIDS

Use a period after initials:

D. H. Lawrence   Dr. N. L. Smithwick

comma (,)

If a date or address has two or more parts, use a comma after each part:

He started working there on July 10, 1991.
His address is 455 Imperial Street, Miami, Florida.

Use a comma to separate items in a series:

She types, files, and answers the phone.

dash (-)

Use a dash between certain numbers:

Her phone number is (760) 555-6577.
Her Social Security number is 114-63-9812.

slash (/)

Use a slash between the month, date, and year:

11/25/66

Use a slash with the abbreviation for the phrase "not applicable":

N/A

parentheses ( )

Use parentheses around the area code:

(760) 555-6577

Can you do it? Look at the partial application form of Tony Anders. With a partner, talk about when Tony used the punctuation marks below. Be sure to use Tony's form as a model when you fill out your own.

(.) periods   (,) commas   (-) dashes
(/) slashes   ( ) parentheses

APPLICATION FOR EMPLOYMENT

1. LAST NAME	FIRST NAME	MIDDLE NAME	2. SOCIAL SECURITY NO.
Anders	Tony	C.	624-54-8192

3. HOME TELEPHONE

(714) 555-6453

4. MESSAGE TELEPHONE

N/A

5. CURRENT ADDRESS (STREET, CITY, STATE, ZIP CODE)

3822 S. Imperial Ave., Apt. 7, Dallas, TX   79399

When you fill out an application form, it is important to use the past tense to describe what you did in jobs that you held in the past.

Last year Tony **worked** as a front desk clerk for three months.
He **answered** the phone.
He **registered** the hotel guests.
He **gave** the guests information about the hotel.

Can you do it? Circle the verbs in the following application that are used incorrectly and rewrite them correctly.

EMPLOYMENT RECORD

FROM	TO	EMPLOYER	TITLE AND RESPONSIBILITIES
9/97	12/97	Quality Hotel	front desk clerk

- I talk to the guests.
- I use a computer to input guest information.
- I take phone messages.

CORRECT VERBS:

_____

_____

_____

Write it up!

PREPARATION: **Organizing information in chronological order**

When you write an employment history, list your jobs in the order in which you held them, with the most recent job first. Look at the form on the next page and then put Tony Anders' employment in the correct order.

DATES FROM (MONTH AND YEAR)	TO (MONTH AND YEAR)	EMPLOYERS
5/91	3/94	Wayne's Shoe Store
9/97	12/97	Quality Motel
2/89	4/91	Best Laundry
4/94	7/97	Holiday Hotel

DATES FROM (MONTH AND YEAR)	TO (MONTH AND YEAR)	EMPLOYERS

PRACTICE

It's time for you to fill out your own application. Pretend that you really want to get this job.

1. With a partner, read through the revision checklist below *before* you fill out the application. The revision checklist will help you be more accurate, complete, and neat.

2. Pick up a job application from a local business. You can get one from a store, school, hospital, or restaurant.

3. Make a copy of the application. Keep the original blank.

4. Fill out the copy of the application. When you have checked all the information, grammar, spelling, and punctuation, copy the information onto the original. Use it as a model the next time you apply for a job.

After you complete your job application, give it to your classmate to read. Your classmate will evaluate your application by completing the revision checklist.

Classmate Revision Checklist

WRITER'S NAME: _____

CHECKER'S NAME: _____

Circle *yes* or *no*.

1. Is the writing neat and legible?   YES   NO
   (If you circled *no*, ask the writer to rewrite it.)

2. Is the application complete?   YES   NO
   (If you circled *no*, highlight the incomplete portion.)

3. Did you understand everything your classmate wrote?   YES   NO
   (If you circled *no*, ask him or her to revise the
   unclear portion.)

4. Are the verbs in the correct tense?   YES   NO
   (If you circled *no*, help the writer correct them.)

5. Are all the words spelled correctly?   YES   NO
   (If you circled *no*, help the writer make corrections.
   If you're not sure of the spelling, use a dictionary.)

6. Do the following words have capital letters?
   (Circle the errors in pencil and ask the writer to
   correct them.)

   ■ proper nouns: names, cities, and states   YES   NO

   ■ names of companies   YES   NO

   ■ names of streets   YES   NO

   ■ first word in a sentence   YES   NO

   ■ days of the week, months of the year   YES   NO

7. Did the writer use the following punctuation marks correctly? (Circle the errors in pencil and ask the writer to correct them.)

- comma: to separate a city from a state   YES   NO

- dashes: with Social Security number   YES   NO

- slash: with "not applicable (N/A)"   YES   NO

8. Does your classmate have work experience?   YES   NO

9. Did your classmate list previous jobs in correct chronological order?(If you circled *no*, ask him or her to redo the list of jobs.)   YES   NO

10. Do you think your classmate will get the job? (If you circled *yes*, why?) (If you circled *no*, why?)   YES   NO

HOW TO SAY IT

Giving suggestions

There are many occasions when you will want to make suggestions to a classmate, coworker, and even at times, a supervisor. Whenever you give advice or make suggestions, it's important to do so in a helpful and constructive manner. Use one of the following expressions to make suggestions helpfully and diplomatically.

> If I were you, I'd . . .
> I suggest that you . . .
> You could . . .
> Why don't you . . . ?
> I recommend that you . . .

Say it! Use these expressions to make suggestions to your classmate as you check his or her job application.

✎ Write it up!

PREPARATION: **Making notes to get organized**

Sometimes there are questions on a job application that need a detailed explanation. Look at the Johnson's Department Store application form and select one of the two questions to answer. Before you write anything on the application, take some time to prepare your answer so that it is clear and well written. First, think about the question. Jot down a few notes about how you might answer it. Review the personal strength words in Chapter 2 and use some in your notes.

Johnson's Department Store
APPLICATION FORM

1. What do you consider to be the most important qualifications of a Johnson's Department Store employee?

   _____

   _____

   _____

2. You are working alone and your shift is due to be over at 6 P.M. The individual who is scheduled to begin working at 6 P.M. does not show up. What would you do?

   _____

   _____

   _____

PRACTICE: **Writing a descriptive paragraph for a job application**

Using your notes, write a paragraph answering one of two questions in the Johnson's Department Store application. Write your paragraph on a separate sheet of paper before copying it on your job application. Remember to write legibly and neatly in pen on an application and to avoid crossing anything out.

EVALUATION: **Monitor and correct your work**

In a group of four students, read your paragraph aloud. After everyone in the group has finished reading, decide who wrote the most effective paragraph. Which words influenced your decision about who would make the best employee?

 O N L I N E !

A. Search. For more tips on filling out employment applications, look up these addresses on the Internet or search on your own:

■ Job Search Part 2:
  Describing your work history: Lesson 10
  http://www.otan.dni.us.webfarm/e-mailproject/rancho/
    intro.htm

■ Effective job applications:
  http://www.uts.edu.au/div/cas/jobappl.html#eja

B. Report. After you find the addresses, tell your classmates or write a brief paragraph on tips for filling out applications effectively.

N O T E

If you don't have a computer or cannot get on the Internet at home, you can:

1. Go to a public library near your home or school. Libraries usually have free Internet access.

2. Find out if you can get on the Internet at your school. Schools often have Internet access.

3. Ask a friend if you can use his or her computer to get on the Internet.

 Check it!

Put a checkmark next to each activity you accomplished in this chapter.

ACADEMIC SKILLS CHECKLIST

Did you . . .

_____ write new vocabulary words in a notebook?

_____ write new grammar rules in a notebook?

_____ interpret and communicate information from the article?

_____ use resources in the classroom, such as a dictionary or a thesaurus?

_____ revise a classmate's application using the revision form?

_____ revise your own application?

_____ make notes to get organized?

_____ write a descriptive paragraph for a job application?

_____ use the Internet to get more information about the topic?

WORK SKILLS CHECKLIST

Did you . . .

_____ work well in your team?

_____ teach other students? What did you teach? _____
_____

_____ do the job that was assigned to you? What was your
job? _____
_____

_____ take individual responsibility by getting an application
form? Where did you get your application? _____
_____

_____ fill out an application completely, neatly, and
accurately?

_____ correctly apply the rules for using capitalization,
punctuation, and the past tense in your job
application?

_____ organize and present the information on your job
application in the correct order?

_____ use common expressions to give advice or suggestions
to someone? What is one expression you used? _____
_____

Chapter 5

Successful Job Interviews

By the end of this chapter, you will be able to:

- Teach classmates information you acquired from an article.

- List ways to build rapport with a job interviewer.

- Use a chart to show the main points of an article.

- Write a summary of an article using information from a chart.

- Revise and edit your own and a classmate's summary.

- Use gerunds as subjects of a sentence.

- Use appropriate language to restate what you said for clarification.

To be successful at school and at work, you need to have certain basic skills and qualities. In this chapter, you will focus on the following skills and qualities:

1. Interpreting and communicating information from an article

2. Organizing information on a chart

3. Evaluating performance

4. Having successful job interviews

5. Responding appropriately to difficult questions in an interview

Talk about it!

1. Have you ever had a job interview? What were some of the questions you were asked?

2. If you wanted to get some advice on how to prepare for a job interview, where would you go?

Take it down!

Your teacher will dictate a paragraph that covers the content and the grammar in this chapter. First, write what you hear. Then check it by using the Dictation Revision Form on the back inside cover.

_____

_____

_____

_____

⬙ Read about it!

Talking about the job application process

With a partner, discuss possible answers to the following questions. Be ready to talk about your answers with the whole group.

1. Answer the following question, which you will sometimes find on a job application: What are your hobbies and interests? _____

   _____

   _____

   _____

   What do you think is the purpose of that question? _____

   _____

   _____

   _____

2. What does the Human Resources Department do? What's another word for Human Resources? If you are working, why might you have to go to that department? _____

   _____

   _____

   _____

3. The most important quality many employers are looking for in an employee is _____

   _____

   _____

   _____

4. The second most important quality employers are looking for is

   _____

   _____

   _____

   _____

A. Read the article. In a group of three students, number 1–3. This is your home group. Split up as follows to read the article:

ALL STUDENTS: Read the first section up to **Common bonds** silently.

ALL #1 STUDENTS: Read the section **Common bonds** together.

ALL #2 STUDENTS: Read the section **Be prepared** together.

ALL #3 STUDENTS: Read the section **Bridge gap** together.

Trying to land a job?
Get interviewer to "fall in love"

CHICAGO – Falling in love is wonderful, and if the person interviewing you for a job thinks you're terrific, you're that much closer to being on the payroll.

"Getting interviewers to 'fall in love' with you refers to job candidates' building rapport, showing right away – assuming you have the job skills – that you are the one who will be the best person to work with, to be part of the team and to have fun with," said Fred W. Ball, executive vice president of Goodrich and Sherwood Associates, a human resource consulting firm in New York.

Ball is the author, with his wife, Barbara B. Ball, of "Killer Interviews," (McGraw-Hill, $10.95). Barbara Ball is a communications consultant and educator.

And one of the Balls' "killer" suggestions is the one about falling in love – "in the business sense only," as they emphasize. Getting the interviewer to adore you starts the moment you walk into the room, they say.

"During the initial chit-chat that occurs you find you have things in common,"

said Ball, who has been with his firm for 11 years and specializes in outplacement.

What often happens to accelerate "falling in love," he says, is as ordinary as a job candidate's mentioning that "he has 'worked with Harry.' Since I know and respect Harry, the candidate has instant credibility."

Common bonds

And if the job seeker also likes tennis, is a volunteer soccer coach, takes photographs as a hobby, and worships the New York Yankees, as Ball does, he feels "an instant rapport, a bond, something to talk about, a commonality of interest."

Ball manages the New York office of the consulting firm and has a staff of about 50. How much of a factor is "falling in love" with the job candidate when he interviews applicants for his staff?

"First of all, I'm looking for someone with the skills to do the job," said Ball, who has a doctorate in educational administration from Columbia University.

"The ability level comes first, and then

I look for someone I can live with ten or 12 hours a day; someone who is optimistic and 100 percent positive that the glass is totally full, not even half-empty; someone with a passion for the job, for life, for meeting people."

Being qualified to do the job is a prerequisite to "falling in love."

Be prepared

"I always look for people who are prepared, who know something about the position they're applying for, the background of the company, and the industry," said Roger Jimenez, a human resources supervisor at Helene Curtis, the Chicago-based hair-care products company.

Jimenez hires technical personnel for the company's business information services, filling such jobs as those for computer analysts, programmers, and technicians.

Bridge gap

Jimenez says to facilitate "falling in love," the job seeker should bridge the gap between the requirements of the job and his or her background. "Don't leave it to the interviewer to figure out why you're there and why you're qualified for the job. Be explicit," he said.

He also urges job seekers to be "energetic, enthusiastic, and positive. The key thing is to be personable and likable."

Source: Carol Kleiman, Chicago Tribune
reprinted in the *San Diego Union-Tribune*, 12-9-96

HOW TO SAY IT

Restating for clarification

If you ever have to teach or train someone, you may need to repeat what you have said in a different way to be sure the person understands you. Use these common expressions when you need to clarify what you meant:

Let me put it another way.

What I mean is . . .

Sorry, let me explain.

Say it! Use these expressions as you work with your classmates to answer the questions about your section of the article.

B. Interpret the article. Work with your classmates to interpret each section of the article.

#1 STUDENTS: **Common bonds.** Work together to find or figure out answers to these questions about your section.

1. According to Fred Ball, it's essential to work with an optimistic person. What is even more important than that? _____

   _____

2. Imagine that you are in a job interview. The interviewer says she likes sports, especially football. What can you say to her to build your relationship? _____

   _____

3. Find synonyms for these words in your section and underline them.
   a. someone looking for a job _____
   b. really likes something or someone _____
   c. a good relationship _____
   d. a connection _____
   e. employees _____

#2 STUDENTS: **Be prepared.** Work together to find or figure out answers to these questions about your section.

1. What characteristics is Jimenez looking for in a candidate?

   _____

2. Imagine that you are in a job interview. The interviewer says that the company sells medical equipment. What can you say to show him that you are prepared for this interview? _____

   _____

3. If Roger Jimenez were interviewing you, which of the jobs he is responsible for would you apply for? _____

4. Find synonyms for these words in your section and underline them.
   a. history _____
   b. personnel department _____

#3 STUDENTS: **Bridge gap.** Work together to find or figure out answers to these questions about your section.

1. What should an applicant do to get an interviewer to like him or her?

   _____

   _____

   _____

   _____

2. Imagine that you are in a job interview. You have been waiting to get an interview for this job for a long time. What is this job? The interviewer asks why he should hire you instead of someone else. What could you say to him or her? _____

   _____

   _____

   _____

3. Find synonyms for these words in your section and underline them.
   a. encourage _____
   b. close the space _____
   c. definite and exact _____
   d. friendly _____

C. Teach each other. Return to your home group and teach your classmates the information you learned in your section.

■ Listen carefully to your classmates as they talk. Ask questions if something isn't clear.

■ When you teach the vocabulary words in your section, show your classmates where the words are and explain the meanings carefully.

■ After you finish teaching each other about your sections, your teacher will give you a short quiz on the entire article.

EVALUATION: **Monitor and correct your work**

A. Quiz. Your teacher will give you a short quiz to see what you learned from your classmates.

B. Group evaluation. Rate the members of your home group (including yourself) according to the questions in the chart.

2 points = very good   1 point = average   0 points = needs improvement

	STUDENT 1	STUDENT 2	STUDENT 3
Did student answer all questions about the sections?			
Did student explain the answers clearly?			
Did student explain all the new vocabulary words?			

1. How well did your group score? What do you need to pay more attention to as a group the next time you do an activity like this one?

2. How did the score you gave yourself compare with the one your classmates gave you? What do you need to pay more attention to as an individual the next time you do an activity like this one?

 O N L I N E !

A. Search. For more advice about successful job interviews, look up these addresses on the Internet or search on your own:

■ Interviewing skills:
http://www.careermosaic.com
click *Career Resource Center*, then *Resource Library*, then *Interviewing Skills*

■ Preparing for a job interview:
http://www.buffnews.com/employ-interview.htm

B. Report. After you find the addresses, tell your classmates or write a brief paragraph about ways to help you prepare for a job interview.

N O T E

If you don't have a computer or cannot get on the Internet at home, you can:

1. Go to a public library near your home or school. Libraries usually have free Internet access.

2. Find out if you can get on the Internet at your school. Schools often have Internet access.

3. Ask a friend if you can use his or her computer to get on the Internet.

✦ Write it up!

PREPARATION: **Using a chart to summarize an article**

Work with a partner. Try to complete the chart without looking back at the article.

- Write the title of the article in the top box of the chart.

- Write the section titles in the three middle boxes of the chart.

- Write specific examples of the key point(s) of each section in the large boxes of the chart. You do not have to write complete sentences.

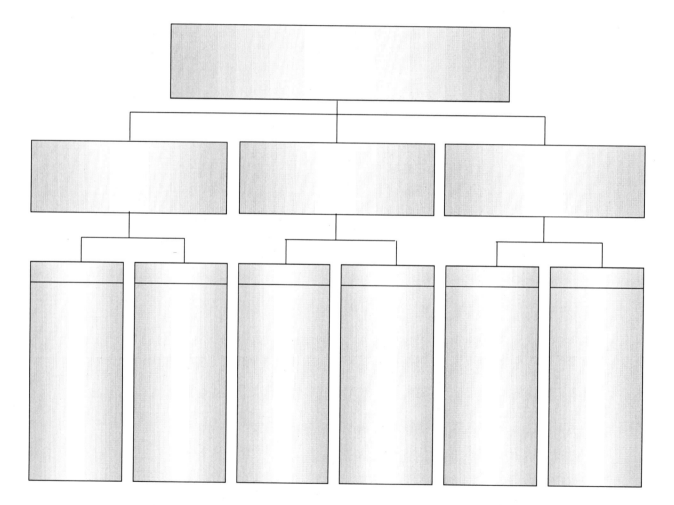

PRACTICE: **Writing a summary**

Summarize the article by using the information in the chart you completed. Write complete sentences. Do not add any new information. The boxes in your chart should contain the main ideas of the article.

EVALUATION: **Monitor and correct your work**

After you finish writing the summary, give both the summary and the chart to a classmate to read. Your classmate will evaluate your summary by completing this revision checklist.

Classmate Revision Checklist

WRITER'S NAME: _____

CHECKER'S NAME: _____

Circle *yes* or *no*.

1. Can you read the writer's handwriting?   YES   NO
   (If you circled *no*, ask the writer to rewrite it.)

2. Did the writer use the information from the chart?   YES   NO

3. Did the writer add information that wasn't in the chart? YES   NO
   (If you circled *yes*, tell the writer to revise the summary
   using only the main points from the chart.)

4. Are the verbs in the correct tense?   YES   NO
   (If you circled *no*, help the writer make corrections.)

5. Are all the words spelled correctly?   YES   NO
   (If you circled *no*, help the writer make corrections.
   If you're not sure of the spelling, use a dictionary.)

6. Does every sentence begin with a capital letter?   YES   NO

7. Does every sentence end with a period?   YES   NO

8. Is the writer's summary similar to yours?   YES   NO
   Explain how it is similar or different.

   _____
   _____
   _____
   _____

PRACTICE: **Answering interview questions**

A. Difficult questions. With a partner or in small groups, discuss these ten questions that are frequently asked in job interviews. Read each question and discuss the best way to answer it. When you have finished, share your responses with the class.

1. I've interviewed people with more experience than you. Why should I hire you?

2. What can you do for this company?

3. What are some of your strengths?

4. What is your greatest weakness?

5. What do you expect as a starting salary?

6. Have you ever had to solve a problem on one of your jobs? What was the problem? How did you resolve it?

7. What do you know about this company (job)?

8. What do you hope to be doing five years from now?

9. Why have you been out of work so long?

10. Do you have any questions for me?

B. Role-play. With a partner, role-play a job interview. Ask and answer as many of the difficult questions you discussed above as you can.

EVALUATION: **Monitor and correct your work**

Role-play the interviews in front of the class. Your classmates will decide who answered the questions the most effectively.

PRACTICE: **Selling yourself**

The article states that job seekers should be energetic, enthusiastic, and positive. During a job interview it's important for the applicant to be personable. In Chapter 2, you practiced talking and writing about your personal strengths. In Chapter 4, you wrote about your job qualifications and strengths. In this chapter, you will practice selling yourself to your classmates. Work in groups of three.

A. Interview each other. Find out about each person's career goals. What qualities and skills does each person have that will help get a job in the field of his or her choice? Get to know each other's strengths.

B. "Sell" a classmate. When you have finished, choose one person from your group and sell him or her to the class or to another group. Use the personal strength adjectives you learned in Chapter 2 and give specific examples.

EXAMPLE: Lee is a busboy now. His long-term career goal is to stay in the restaurant business, working his way up to assistant manager, maybe even someday opening up his own restaurant. He's a team player. When a coworker isn't there, he pitches in to get the job done. He doesn't say, "That isn't my job." He tries to help out whenever he can. Everyone likes him because he is helpful and always in a good mood, even when things get really busy.

EVALUATION: **Monitor and correct your work**

Discuss whether or not you would "hire" your classmates. Suggest additional skills and qualities that each one should develop for his or her particular career goal.

Practical grammar: Using gerunds as subjects

A gerund is the **-ing** form of a verb (**eating, typing**) used as a noun. A gerund is often used alone or with other nouns as the subject of a sentence:

> **Keyboarding** is an essential skill at school and at work.
>
> **Answering** the phone politely is important in business.

The subject of the first sentence is **keyboarding**. What is the subject of

the second sentence? _____

Can you do it? Find gerunds in the article you read.

1. Read the first sentence of the article and write it here. Circle the gerund.

   _____

2. Scan the article for two more gerunds. Write the sentences here and circle the gerunds.

   _____

   _____

An infinitive is sometimes used as the subject of a sentence, but it is more common to use a gerund. Get in the habit of using gerunds instead of infinitives as subjects:

To use a computer is an important skill.
INFINITIVE

Using a computer is an important skill.
GERUND

Not using a computer will slow you down.
GERUND

Can you do it? Replace the infinitives used as subjects with gerunds.

1. To get stuck in traffic on the way to school happens sometimes.

   _____

2. To teach a coworker how to use a new machine helps you learn.

   _____

3. To have a meeting on Friday afternoon isn't a very good idea.

   _____

4. Not to proofread a letter before you send it is careless.

   _____

5. To learn a language takes a long time.

   _____

A. Gerunds as subjects. Complete each sentence with a gerund. Use your own opinions.

1. _____ is difficult for women.

2. _____ is impossible for men.

3. _____ relaxes me at the end of a day.

4. _____ isn't good for you.

5. _____ occurs frequently in an office.

6. _____ takes a long time.

7. _____ is an American custom.

8. _____ is an important decision in one's life.

9. _____ is against the law.

10. _____ isn't polite.

11. _____ makes me homesick.

12. _____ makes me nervous.

13. _____ is one skill of an automotive technician.

14. _____ is important for children.

15. _____

    (Write your own sentence using a gerund as subject.)

B. Team competition using gerunds. Divide into two teams. You have five minutes to make sentences with gerunds as subjects using the words below. Your teacher will call one person from each team to write their sentences on the board. The whole team will get points if:

■ the gerund is spelled correctly.

■ the sentence is grammatically correct and makes sense.

If necessary, refer to Chapter 2 to review the spelling rules.

plan	get	job
open	begin	study
write	apply	earn
stay		

 # Check it!

Put a checkmark next to each activity you accomplished in this chapter.

ACADEMIC SKILLS CHECKLIST

Did you . . .

_____ write new vocabulary words in a notebook?

_____ write new grammar rules in a notebook?

_____ listen to your classmates and ask them questions?

_____ think creatively about the topic before you read the article by discussing the questions with a partner?

_____ interpret and communicate information from an article?

_____ use resources in the classroom, such as a dictionary or a thesaurus?

_____ write a summary of the article?

_____ evaluate a classmate's summary using the revision form?

_____ use gerunds correctly?

_____ use the Internet to get more information about the topic?

WORK SKILLS CHECKLIST

Did you . . .

_____ work collaboratively in your team?

_____ teach other students? What did you teach other
students? _____

_____

_____ learn about having a successful job interview? What is
one important thing you learned about interviewing for
a job? _____

_____

_____ think creatively about the article before you read it with
clues from the teacher?

_____ assess your own and your teammates' performance in
acquiring and communicating information?

_____ organize your ideas on a chart?

_____ use expressions to restate what someone said for
clarification? What is one expression you used? _____

_____

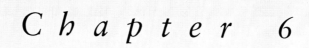

Chapter 6

Small Talk at the Water Cooler

OBJECTIVES

By the end of this chapter, you will be able to:

■ Teach classmates information you acquired from an article.

■ Demonstrate ways to be more approachable in social situations.

■ Give topics that are appropriate for making small talk.

■ Demonstrate good listening techniques.

■ Write a paragraph from topic categories.

■ Revise and edit your own and a classmate's paragraph.

■ Ask and answer grammatically correct open-ended questions.

■ Use appropriate language to end a conversation.

To be successful at school and at work, you need to have certain basic skills and qualities. In this chapter, you will focus on the following skills and qualities:

1. Analyzing and interpreting information

2. Making small talk

3. Organizing information

4. Evaluating performance

Talk about it!

1. What is small talk? Why is it important?

2. In your culture, what kinds of things would you talk about to get acquainted with someone? Are there any topics that you would probably not discuss with a new acquaintance? Any questions you would not ask?

Take it down!

Your teacher will dictate a paragraph that covers the content and the grammar in this chapter. First, listen to what you hear. Then check it by using the Dictation Revision Form on the back inside cover.

_____

_____

_____

_____

◈ Read about it!

PREPARATION: **Brainstorming to define a problem and solve it**

Brainstorming is a good way to come up with new ideas or a solution to a problem. When a group of people brainstorm, they call out or write down all their ideas about a topic or problem. In groups of four, you will first brainstorm to discover the problem in the pictures and then to come up with solutions.

A. What's the problem? First call out answers to the questions. Then decide on the best answer to each question.

1. Where is Chung?

2. What is she doing?

3. What do you think is wrong with her? Why?

B. What's the solution? In groups of four, give each student a number from 1 to 4.

STUDENT 1: Take out a sheet of blank paper and write an answer to question 1. When the teacher gives the signal, pass the paper to Student 2.

STUDENT 2: Write another answer to question 1. When the teacher gives the signal, pass the paper to Student 3.

When each student in your group has written an answer to question 1, repeat the process for questions 2 and 3.

1. What common subjects are appropriate for making small talk in your country?

2. Give at least one example of an open-ended question appropriate for making small talk.

3. What common expressions do people use when the conversation is over and it's time to leave?

NOTE

A closed-ended question requires only a **yes** or **no** answer:

> Do you live near here?

An open-ended question requires a longer response. These questions often begin with **Wh-** words **(who, where, when, what, why)**:

> Where do you live?

PRACTICE: **Acquiring and interpreting information**

A. Read the article. Remain in your group of four students.

STUDENTS 1 AND 2: Read the sections **Keep the conversation going** and **Ask and ask and ask.**

STUDENTS 3 AND 4: Read the sections **Fear of rejection** and **Make yourself approachable.**

What Do You Say After You Say Hello?

Keep the conversation going

Conversation should be like a ball bouncing back and forth with no one holding on too long or passing it too quickly. Show interest in the person you are talking to. Making conversation includes being a good listener. Ask open-ended questions that leave room for explanation. Closed-ended questions that bring about one-word answers are conversation killers. People like to talk about themselves and like to have others show interest in them.

Ask and ask and ask

One sure way to get anyone talking is to inquire about their favorite subject – themselves. "Do you like your job?" "Have you lived in this neighborhood long?" Open-ended questions are best because they can't be answered with a simple yes or no. "With three young kids, how are you able to stay in such good shape?" (Flattering people is also a painless way to relax them, and keep them chatting.) And to keep the conversation going, listen to the answers they give you. They'll give you your next question.

Fear of rejection

We all have this. Remember, being rejected by someone who doesn't know you means nothing. It is merely a reflection of what the other person is feeling at the time or perceives is right for them. Maybe you remind them of someone else. Or there may be something else in their lives at the moment that has nothing to do with you. Don't take it personally.

Make yourself approachable

Remember the letters in the word SOFTEN.

- ➤ **S**mile
- ➤ **O**pen body posture
- ➤ **F**orward lean
- ➤ **T**ouch (not acceptable for men, but usually acceptable for women)
- ➤ **E**ye contact
- ➤ **N**atural behavior

About touching: men should generally avoid this especially early on, because it implies aggression. That is not the first impression that you want to make. But for women, just a little tap on the shoulder or arm can be a good way to relax the person you are with.

Source: Adapted from "What do you say after you say hello?" by Susan Downing, and "Successful Mingling" *Good Housekeeping*, The Hearst Corporation, December 1995.

B. Interpret the article. Work with your classmates to interpret each section of the article.

STUDENTS 1 AND 2: **Keep the conversation going** and **Ask and ask and ask**

1. How does the writer describe the way a good conversation should be?

   _____

   _____

2. There are two partners in a conversation. One is the speaker. Who is the other one?

   _____

   _____

3. What would you say to inquire about my family?

   _____

   _____

4. Say something flattering to your partner and write it here.

   _____

   _____

STUDENTS 3 AND 4: **Fear of rejection** and **Make yourself approachable**

1. Sometimes people won't want to talk to you. Give a few reasons why this might happen.

   _____

   _____

2. Have a conversation without words. Act out the facial expressions and body language that will make you approachable.

3. Have another conversation without words. This time, act out the facial expressions and body language that will make you unapproachable.

C. Teach each other. Share the information you learned in your section with each other.

STUDENT 1: Teach Student 3. Then switch roles.
STUDENT 2: Teach Student 4. Then switch roles.

After you have explained your sections to each other, your teacher will go over the answers with the whole class.

EVALUATION: **Monitor and correct your work**

At work there are occasions when your supervisor might ask you to evaluate your job performance or the performance of a coworker. Rate the members of your group (including yourself) according to the questions in the chart.

2 points = very good   1 point = average   0 points = needs improvement

	STUDENT 1	STUDENT 2	STUDENT 3	STUDENT 4
Did student answer all questions about the sections?				
Did student explain the answers clearly?				
Did student help other students in the group?				

1. How well did your group score? What do you need to pay more attention to as a group the next time you do an activity like this one?

2. How did the score you gave yourself compare with the one your classmates gave you? What do you need to pay more attention to as an individual the next time you do an activity like this one?

A. Search. For more information about making small talk, look up these addresses on the Internet, or search on your own:

- Successful mingling – small talk:
  http://homearts.com/gh/betterw/12bwmib4.htm

- Successful mingling – ask and ask:
  http://homearts.com/gh/betterw/12bwmib5.htm

- Successful mingling – exit gracefully:
  http://homearts.com/gh/betterw/12bwmib6.htm

B. Report. After you find the addresses, tell your classmates or write a brief paragraph about what you might say the next time you have to make small talk, either at work, school, or in social situations.

N O T E

If you don't have a computer or cannot get on the Internet at home, you can:

1. Go to a public library near your home or school. Libraries usually have free Internet access.

2. Find out if you can get on the Internet at your school. Schools often have Internet access.

3. Ask a friend if you can use his or her computer to get on the Internet.

PREPARATION: **Practicing effective listening**

Talking is only one part of communicating. An equally important (and sometimes forgotten) part of a two-way exchange is listening. Here are some techniques that will make you a better listener.

TECHNIQUE 1: Have good eye contact with the person who is talking.

TECHNIQUE 2: Pay attention to the speaker. Don't spend time thinking about how you're going to respond to the person.

TECHNIQUE 3: Ask a question occasionally, or paraphrase what you heard.

TECHNIQUE 4: Don't fidget while the other person is speaking.

TECHNIQUE 5: Make listening sounds to show you are really listening (**uh-huh, yes, I see, oh really?**).

TECHNIQUE 6: If necessary, write things down. Don't keep your head in a notebook, but jot down quick notes.

TECHNIQUE 7: Don't be afraid to ask the person to repeat something or to slow down.

Identifying and using listening techniques

A. Write the number of the listening technique on the previous page next to the appropriate example.

_____ 1. You avoid moving around a lot while the other person talks.

_____ 2. You tell the speaker you can't hear him or her.

_____ 3. You say what the other person said, in different words.

_____ 4. You tell the speaker to say again something that you didn't understand.

_____ 5. You look at the speaker's eyes.

_____ 6. You write down important things to remember.

_____ 7. You concentrate on what the speaker says, not on what you are going to say next.

_____ 8. You say, "Um-humm, oh?" while you are listening.

B. What are your skills as a listener? Interview a partner about his or her listening skills and check the appropriate boxes.

	NEVER	SOMETIMES	OFTEN	ALWAYS
Do you . . .				
1. maintain eye contact when a person is talking?				
2. pay attention when a person is speaking?				
3. worry about what you're going to say while the other person is talking?				
4. fidget when another person talks?				
5. make listening sounds when another person talks?				
6. take notes and jot down important information when necessary?				
7. ask a person to repeat something or slow down?				

1. Which listening skills are hard for you?

2. Which ones do you often or always use?

3. Share your responses with a partner and talk about which skills you want to improve.

C. Practice listening well. In groups of three, give each student a number from 1 to 3.

STUDENT 1: Speak for about 2–3 minutes. Talk about the first day of meeting people: at school to new classmates, on the job to new coworkers, in your neighborhood to your neighbors, etc.

STUDENT 2: Listen well, using the tips you learned.

STUDENT 3: Observe the listener and fill out the evaluation checklist.

Tell the listener how his or her listening skills were. Take turns doing this activity so that each team member has a chance to speak, listen, and observe.

LISTENING EVALUATION CHECKLIST

Circle *yes* or *no*.

1. Did the listener look at the speaker?	YES	NO
2. Did the listener ask any questions?	YES	NO
3. Did the listener fidget?	YES	NO
4. Did the listener make any listening sounds?	YES	NO
5. Did the listener ask the speaker to repeat anything?	YES	NO

Practical grammar: Asking questions

You read that asking open-ended questions is one of the best ways to make small talk. **Yes/no questions** are questions that can be answered by saying **yes** or **no**, without giving additional information. In yes/no questions, your voice rises at the end of the question.

Does Teresa work downtown?
Yes, she does.   OR   **No,** she doesn't.

Information (or **open-ended**) **questions** usually use a question word, such as **where, when, why, who, what, which, whose,** or **how** in the question. Answers to information questions contain specific facts, explanations, or other information:

Where does Teresa work?
She works downtown in an electronics company.

FORM

Study the pattern of question formation for yes/no questions:

AUXILIARY/ HELPING VERB	SUBJECT	MAIN VERB	
Does	Sara	work	at night?
Do	you	study	every day?
Did	the manager	go	to the staff party?
Will	you	turn off	the computer?
Can	the student	finish	the assignment?

Study the pattern of question formation for open-ended questions:

QUESTION WORD	AUXILIARY/ HELPING VERB	SUBJECT	VERB	
Where	does	Sara	work?	
What topics	can	we	discuss?	
Where	did	the manager	put	the report?
Who	will	you	go	with?
When	do	you	study?	

Can you do it? Indicate which items are yes/no questions and which ones are information questions by circling Y/N or I.

1. Y/N   I   What are those people talking about?

2. Y/N   I   Is the staff party a pot-luck supper?

3. Y/N   I   Who will answer the phone?

4. Y/N   I   Didn't you remember to call the repairman?

5. Y/N   I   How did the accident happen?

6. Y/N   I   Were the managers satisfied with the work?

7. Y/N   I   When are you going to finish the report?

8. Y/N   I   Why don't you come to the cafeteria with us?

9. Y/N   I   Does the boardroom have an easel?

10. Y/N   I   Can you type the rest of the minutes later?

PRACTICE

A. What's the question? Make open-ended (information) questions. Use **where, why, when,** or **what.** When you have finished, check a classmate's paper. If you have any differences, discuss them and decide who is correct.

EXAMPLE: Why did you leave work early?
I left because I had an appointment.

1. _____?
I'll be here tomorrow by 8:30.

2. _____?
John usually eats lunch in the cafeteria.

3. _____?
I'm going to pick up the brochures tomorrow.

4. _____?
I think basketball is my favorite sport.

5. _____?
It's cheaper.   OR   I bring my lunch because I want to save money.

B. Preparing for small talk. Before you begin making small talk, write at least four questions that would be appropriate for initiating small talk. Use the topics below to give you ideas. Share the questions you have written with a partner. Check each others' questions to make sure they are grammatically correct.

Topics

FAMILY: brothers and sisters, parents, childhood, home

FRIENDS: many? few? male and female? activities you do when you're together

TRAVEL: favorite vacation, countries visited, places you'd like to visit

EDUCATION: best subjects at school, degrees, goals

CAREER GOALS: job now, job desired in the future, skills

FREE TIME: sports, TV, hobbies, weekend activities, movies

H O W   T O   S A Y   I T

Ending a conversation politely

What do you say when you are in the middle of a conversation and you have to leave or, for some other reason, end the conversation? You may use one of these expressions to let the other person know that you're ready to leave and end the conversation in a polite and smooth manner:

I'd love to continue this conversation, but . . .
Sorry, but I think I should be going now.
Well, I've got to go now.
I'm sorry I have to rush off like this.
Well, I don't want to take up any more of your time.

Then, when the person you are speaking with understands that you are leaving, close the conversation by saying good-bye:

Speak to you soon.
Take care.
Take it easy.
See you later.

Say it! Use these expressions to end the conversations you will have in Exercise C.

C. Making small talk. Practice starting and ending conversations. Get into two groups. Students in Group A will hold a pen or pencil to differentiate themselves from students in Group B.

GROUP A STUDENTS: Using one of the topics below, ask open-ended questions of a Group B student. You will have two minutes. When your teacher signals that the time is up, end the conversation with one of the expressions you learned.

GROUP B STUDENTS: Do not speak until a student in Group A approaches and starts the conversation by asking you a question. Answer your classmate's questions and let him or her end the conversation.

After several conversations, change groups.

GROUP B STUDENTS: Now it's your turn to ask the questions and end the conversation.

GROUP A STUDENTS: Answer your classmates' questions.

 Write it up!

PREPARATION: **Using categories to organize your writing**

Using the categories in this chart as a guide, jot down some of the things you learned about your classmates in your notebook.

NAME	FAMILY	FRIENDS	TRAVEL	EDUCATION	CAREER GOALS	FREE TIME
___	___	___	___	___	___	___
___	___	___	___	___	___	___
___	___	___	___	___	___	___
___	___	___	___	___	___	___
___	___	___	___	___	___	___
___	___	___	___	___	___	___
___	___	___	___	___	___	___

PRACTICE: **Writing a paragraph**

Using the notes you made in the chart, write a paragraph about the most interesting things you learned about your classmates during your conversations with them. Make your paragraph organized and coherent by following the categories of the chart to write your descriptions.

EVALUATION: **Monitor and correct your work**

Read your paragraphs in front of the class. Find out if your classmates agree with what you wrote about them.

 # Check it!

Put a checkmark next to each activity you accomplished in this chapter.

ACADEMIC SKILLS CHECKLIST

Did you . . .

_____ write new vocabulary words in a notebook?

_____ write new grammar rules in a notebook?

_____ interpret and communicate information from the article?

_____ use resources inside the classroom, such as a dictionary or a thesaurus?

_____ ask open-ended questions correctly? What is one open-ended question you asked? _____

_____

_____ use categories to organize your writing?

_____ write a paragraph describing what you learned about your classmates when you made small talk with them? What is one thing you learned about a classmate? _____

_____

_____ use the Internet to get more information about the topic?

Did you . . .

_____ brainstorm with your group to define and solve a problem?

_____ teach your classmates the information in your section of the article?

_____ evaluate your own and your group's performance?

_____ show sociability by making small talk?

_____ allocate enough time to ask and answer questions during the small talk activity?

_____ use expressions to end a conversation politely? What is one expression you used? _____

_____

_____ practice being a good listener?

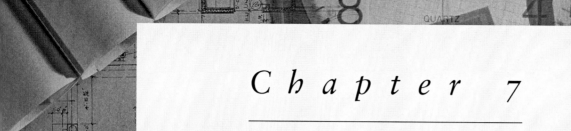

Chapter 7

Improving Relationships at Work

By the end of this chapter, you will be able to:

■ Teach classmates information you acquired from an article.

■ Give solutions for dealing with bothersome coworkers or classmates.

■ Write a letter of advice.

■ Revise and edit your letter.

■ Do basic math (percentages).

■ Interpret and make a bar graph.

■ Use modal auxiliaries to show respect, give advice, and express preferences.

■ Use appropriate language to give advice.

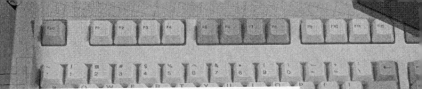

To be successful at school and at work, you need to have certain basic skills and qualities. In this chapter, you will focus on the following skills and qualities:

1. Figuring out definitions by using contextual clues

2. Paraphrasing the main points of an article

3. Interpreting bar graphs

4. Computing percentages

Talk about it!

1. Have you ever worked with a person who had a bad habit? Have you ever had a classmate who did something that annoyed you?

2. With the whole class, make a list of bad habits that you have experienced or know about. Briefly discuss why each bad habit is a problem.

Take it down!

Your teacher will dictate a paragraph that covers the content and the grammar in this chapter. First write what you hear. Then check it by using the Dictation Revision Form on the back inside cover.

_____

_____

_____

_____

_____

◈ Read about it!

PREPARATION: **Getting your ideas down**

In a group of four students, take two minutes to write about your experience with a coworker or classmate who had a bad habit. Write as much as you can. Use the following questions as a guide. Don't worry about spelling and grammar. Get your ideas on the paper as they come to you.

1. What bad habit did your coworker or classmate have? _____

   _____

   _____

   _____

   _____

2. What did you do about it? Did you ask the person to stop? Did you keep it to yourself? _____

   _____

   _____

   _____

   _____

3. Did you tell your supervisor or your teacher? _____

   _____

   _____

   _____

   _____

Discuss the similarities and differences in your group's experiences. How did each of you react to the person with a bad habit?

PRACTICE: **Guessing from context**

A. Read the article. Remain in your group of four students. Silently read the article. Try not to use your dictionaries the first time you read. By reading the sentence and the rest of the paragraph, you should be able to guess the meanings of new words.

BAD 👁👁 HABITS

How do you tell coworkers they're driving you crazy?

Annoyances

Do you have a coworker whose voice is loud enough to rattle the ceiling tiles loose? How about one whose body odor is so strong you can smell him three cubicles away? Or the busybody who listens to all of your conversations and then injects her own running commentary about your life?

As we spend more hours on the job, our work relationships become increasingly more important. Being cramped in 6 x 6 cubicles is enough to make anyone crabby, but having to smell your cubicle mate's stinky garlic bagel or listen to your colleague's electric letter opener can make your blood boil.

Yet many workers hold their grievances in, fearing confrontation. They'd rather suffer in silence.

Approaching your colleagues

Well, suffer no more. For advice on reforming your colleagues, we went directly to the big names in the world of good manners – Letitia Baldrige, renowned author and business etiquette expert, and Nancy Tuckerman, coauthor of *The Amy Vanderbilt Complete Book of Etiquette*, as well as specialists in conflict resolution. (We tried Miss Manners, too, but she didn't return our calls. Not very polite of her, wouldn't you say?)

Lack of courtesy in the workplace wasn't a surprise to any of them.

"In this culture, we are moving away from treating people respectfully," said Marjorie Hansen Shaevitz, a La Jolla workplace consultant. "We should get back to being polite to each other."

And that means approaching your colleague politely – but firmly – about minor annoyances before they become major aggravations.

"Instead of telling the truth (about how a coworker's habit annoys you), the negative feelings build up and you begin to have thoughts that the person is a jerk and is purposely annoying you," said Danni Burton, a San Jose consultant who leads workshops on interpersonal skills. "Most likely, the person sitting on the other side is probably totally unaware of what's going on."

The experts say the direct approach is best.

But no one likes criticism, and bringing up your gripes about someone can be a touchy situation You don't want to make your colleague go on the defensive and create an even more uncomfortable work environment. After all, you have to spend eight hours a day or more with this person.

Good advice

Here's some advice on how to approach your office mate about his or her annoying habits:

1. Practice what you're going to say to your colleague. Go through a dry run with your spouse or another coworker.

2. Watch your tone of voice, the vocabulary you use and your posture. Be calm and collected when approaching your colleague. Don't use phrases such as "You ought to" or "You always do such and such."

3. Use the "I" instead of "you" approach. Say something like, "I'd appreciate it if you would keep your voice down. I'm having a hard time concentrating." That's more palatable than "You talk too loud. Please be quiet" or "Shut up."

4. Don't blame. Don't put the burden on your coworker to change. Take a conflict-resolution approach by offering to work together on problems. Solicit help from the coworker so that he or she doesn't feel like the one who is "wrong."

"Most people won't even know how their actions are affecting others," said Frank Delfiugo, a consultant for the Growth and Leadership Center in Mountain View, Calif., who works with corporations on team building.

5. Give your colleague a chance to give his or her point of view. This process builds understanding between the two parties. "Go one on one and get it all out," said Baldrige, who is based in Washington. "But let the other person get their grievances out first."

6. Show empathy. Try to understand why a person behaves the way he or she does. Ask questions. A loud talker may have a hearing problem that you are unaware of.

7. Ask your colleague out for coffee or to lunch to let him or her know that you didn't mean anything personal by your request. "Shake hands at the end, and agree to get along better," Baldrige said. "Always end on a positive note."

8. Don't get discouraged if the discussion with your colleague doesn't bring immediate results. You may have to bring up the topic again later. "What most people do is ask one time, and if change doesn't happen, they get frustrated and give up," Delfiugo said.

9. If trying to work a situation out with an individual doesn't help, consult your company's human resources department for advice. Some situations may be too serious for one individual to handle.

Source: Sherri Eng, Knight Ridder/Tribune
Information Services
Reprinted in the *San Diego Union-Tribune* 3/25/96

ONLINE!

A. Search. For more about how to handle problems with people in the workplace, look up these addresses on the Internet or search on your own:

- Face-to-face communication:
  http://www.rt66.com/~mikep/Good.Words/

- How to communicate with Hispanic employees:
  http://www.LaCalle.com

B. Report. After you find the addresses, tell your classmates or write a brief paragraph about some things you can say to give constructive criticism.

NOTE

If you don't have a computer or cannot get on the Internet at home, you can:

1. Go to a public library near your home or school. Libraries usually have free Internet access.

2. Find out if you can get on the Internet at your school. Schools often have Internet access.

3. Ask a friend if you can use his or her computer to get on the Internet.

B. Work together. In groups of four students, give each student a number from 1 to 4.

STUDENTS 1 AND 2: Work together on numbers 1–5.

STUDENTS 3 AND 4: Work together on numbers 6–10.

With your partner, write synonyms (words with similar meanings) for the words in your sentences. Then rewrite each sentence with your new word. If you need additional clues, use the bank of synonyms below. Some words may be used more than once.

crowded	should	compassion
annoying you	complaints	rehearsal
annoyances	responsibility	
put anyone in a bad mood	make you angry	

1. How do you tell coworkers they're *driving you crazy*?

   synonym for *driving you crazy*: _____

   sentence with new expression: _____

2. Being *cramped* in 6 x 6 cubicles is enough to *make anyone crabby*.

   synonym for *cramped*: _____

   synonym for *make anyone crabby*: _____

   sentence with new word and expression: _____

   _____

3. Having to smell your cubicle mate's stinky garlic bagel or listen to your colleague's electric letter opener can *make your blood boil*.

   synonym for *make your blood boil*: _____

   sentence with new expression: _____

   _____

4. Many workers hold their *grievances* in, fearing confrontation.

   synonym for *grievances*: _____

   sentence with new word: _____

   _____

5. And that means approaching your colleague politely – but firmly – about minor annoyances before they become major *aggravations*.

   synonym for *aggravations*: _____

   sentence with new word: _____

   _____

6. But no one likes criticism, and bringing up your *gripes* about someone can be a touchy situation.

   synonym for *gripes*: _____

   sentence with new word: _____

   _____

7. *Go through a dry run* with your spouse or another coworker.

   synonym for *go through a dry run*: _____

   sentence with new word: _____

   _____

8. Don't use phrases such as "You *ought to*" or "You always do such and such."

   synonym for *ought to*: _____

   sentence with new word: _____

   _____

9. Don't blame. Don't put the *burden* on your coworker to change.

synonym for *burden*: _____

sentence with new word: _____

_____

10. Show *empathy*. Try to understand why a person behaves the way he or she does.

synonym for *empathy*: _____

sentence with new word: _____

_____

When you have finished, look up the words in the dictionary to see if you are correct.

C. Teach each other. Share the new vocabulary words you learned with each other.

STUDENT 1: Explain your words to Student 3. Then switch roles.

STUDENT 2: Explain your words to Student 4. Then switch roles.

PRACTICE: **Interpreting and communicating**

A. Interpret the article. Work with your classmates to interpret each section of the article.

STUDENTS 1 AND 2: **Annoyances**

The writer describes three annoying things that could happen at work. Discuss these three things with your partner. Write down the annoyances in your own words.

1. _____

2. _____

3. _____

STUDENTS 3 AND 4: **Approaching your colleagues**

1. Whom did the author consult about advice on changing the habits of coworkers? _____

2. Why did the author go to these specific people? _____

   _____

3. What do the experts on good manners think employees should do when a coworker is driving them crazy? _____

   _____

4. Do the experts think people annoy their coworkers on purpose? Explain your answer. _____

   _____

B. Teach each other. Teach a classmate the information you learned in your section. Listen carefully to your classmates as they speak. Ask questions if something isn't clear.

STUDENT 1: Explain your section to Student 3. Then switch roles.

STUDENT 2: Explain your section to Student 4. Then switch roles.

ALL STUDENTS: **Good advice**

The writer gives nine suggestions for approaching a coworker about an annoying habit. Read the advice carefully. With a highlighter pen, highlight the key words for each suggestion given. **Paraphrase** a few of the suggestions, that is, tell them to your group in your own words by looking only at the key words you highlighted.

EVALUATION: **Monitor and correct your work**

A. Explain. Remain in your group of four students. Your teacher will call out two numbers: a student number from 1–4 and a number from 1–9 that corresponds to the list of advice in the article. The student that the teacher calls must explain the suggestion to his or her team by looking at the highlighted words only.

B. Think about it. Look back at what you wrote before you read the article. Now that you have read the article, how would you handle the annoying classmate or coworker you wrote about?

Practical grammar: Modal auxiliaries

Modal auxiliaries are helping verbs. They express the speaker's attitude about an action. Modal auxiliary verbs are very common in English.

1. Giving advice with *should, ought to* and *had better*

In the article, you read:

> We **should** get back to being polite to each other.
> Don't use phrases [with your coworkers] such as **You ought to . . .**

■ **Should** and **ought to** mean the same thing—they express advice. They mean, "This is a good idea." or "This is my advice to you."

■ **Should** and **ought to** can be softened with "Perhaps you should . . ." or "Maybe you ought to . . ."

■ **Ought to** is often pronounced "otta" in spoken English. You don't have to say "otta," but you have to understand when other people do. Remember, you may use "otta" when you speak, but never when you write. You must write **ought to.**

■ **Had better is** also used to give advice, but it is stronger than **should** or **ought to.** It is used to give warnings and to advise the listener that bad consequences might happen.

> You **had better** finish the report, or the supervisor will be angry.

■ The contraction **'d** may be substituted for **had:**

> You'**d** better finish your report, or the supervisor will be angry.

■ Use **should** or **had better** rather than **ought** when telling someone what not to do. The negative is usually not used with **ought:**

> You **should not** miss this meeting.
> You'**d better not** be late!

■ **Should not** is often contracted to **shouldn't:**

> You **shouldn't** miss this meeting.

2. Using *would* in imaginary *if*-sentences and polite requests

■ Imaginary if-sentences express situations that are not true at the present time. They may be used as an indirect way of giving advice.

INDIRECT:	I **would** appreciate it if you **would** keep your voice down.
DIRECT:	You **should** keep your voice down.
INDIRECT:	I **would** talk to my supervisor if I were you.
DIRECT:	You **ought to** talk to your supervisor.

■ **Would** is also used to make polite requests. It is formal and used as a sign of respect with strangers or people in authority.

FORMAL/POLITE:	**Would** you help me carry these boxes?
INFORMAL:	**Can** you help me carry these boxes?

3. Expressing preferences with *would rather*

■ Find the sentence with the phrase **would rather** in the third paragraph of the article and write it below (remember that **I + would** contracts to **I'd**):

_____

■ The phrase **would rather** is used to express what a person would prefer to do. Compare:

I'd **prefer** to work at a bank.
I'd **rather** work at a bank.

The two sentences above mean the same thing. After **prefer,** use **to**; after **would rather**, use the simple form of the verb.

4. Summary: Uses of modal auxiliary (helping) verbs

should	give advice
ought to	give advice
had better	give advice/warning
would + if	give advice indirectly
would	make polite request
would rather	express preference

■ Notice the form of the modal auxiliaries (helping verbs) and the words that follow them in two of the sentences from the article:

> We **should** get back to being polite to each other.
> They**'d rather** suffer in silence.

■ To form a statement, use the modal + the simple form of the main verb.

■ Modals do not change form to agree with the subject. There is no final -s or -es after a modal:

> He **should** tell his colleagues what is bothering him.
> She **would rather** work later and finish the report.

Can you do it? Circle the modal auxiliaries. Underline the main verbs.

1. When you get the application, the first thing you should do is read it thoroughly.

2. She ought to answer the phone very politely at work.

3. Maryann had better call if she's going to be absent.

4. They'd rather hold in their grievances than confront the boss.

5. Would you unlock the cabinet for me? My hands are full.

H O W   T O   S A Y   I T

Giving advice

Frequently at school or at work you will have to give advice to someone. It is important to give advice politely, or the person might think you are bossy or a know-it-all. Use these expressions to give advice politely.

Maybe you should . . .   I recommend that you . . .
Perhaps you ought to . . .   It might be a good idea to . . .
Why don't you . . . ?   If I were you, I would . . .

Say it! Use these expressions to make polite suggestions for handling the situations in Exercise A.

PRACTICE

A. Give advice. With a partner, practice giving advice politely.

STUDENT 1: Read each situation aloud.

STUDENT 2: Make a polite suggestion for handling the situation. Use **should, ought to,** or **had better.**

STUDENT 1: End the conversation by making a comment on what your partner told you.

Switch roles.

EXAMPLE: STUDENT 1: The supervisor asked Sharon to file the invoices before 4:00. It's 3:45 and she hasn't done it yet.

STUDENT 2: She**'d better** file those papers before she does anything else.

STUDENT 1: You're right. She **should** do what her boss told her and finish her other work later.

Other possible answers for Student 2:

She **ought to** file those papers before she does anything else.
She**'d better not** wait to file those invoices.
She **shouldn't** wait to file those invoices.

1. The health department is going to inspect the restaurant where you work.
2. Your partner can't stop yawning.
3. I'm probably going to be late tomorrow because I have to take a friend to the airport.
4. The company is offering a free computer class to all employees who sign up within a week.
5. Your library book is due tomorrow.
6. It's Alexander's turn to bring donuts to the meeting on Friday.
7. I don't feel very well. Maybe I'm getting the flu.
8. Tomorrow the banks close early because of the holiday but I have to cash my check.
9. You have a job interview tomorrow but you don't know much about the company.
10. Terry wants to go to cosmetology school but she doesn't have enough money for the tuition.

B. Express your preferences. With a partner, ask and answer these questions to find out about each other's preferences. Then ask and answer the question "Why?" to find out the reason for each other's preferences.

EXAMPLE: STUDENT 1: Which would you rather do, work in a bank or a hotel?

STUDENT 2: I'd rather work in a hotel.

STUDENT 1: Why?

STUDENT 2: Because I can meet more people in a hotel.

Which would you rather do . . . ?

1. learn how to use an IBM well/learn how to use a Macintosh well?

2. be an accountant/be a receptionist/be an auto mechanic?

3. use a spreadsheet/use a ledger form?

4. work alone/work with a group of people?

5. work for someone/be your own boss?

6. work in a large company/work in a small company?

7. read a manual for instructions/troubleshoot?

8. get a promotion/get an award for employee of the month?

9. use hand tools/use computers?

10. speak your native language during the break/speak English during the break?

 Write it up!

PREPARATION: **Brainstorming annoyances in the classroom and on the job**

Brainstorming is a good way to pool everyone's ideas and experiences. In your group of four, choose one student to be the recorder. Write down as many annoying things that you can think of that happen in the classroom or on the job. Think of previous classes or jobs you have had or heard about or your children's classes.

PRACTICE: **Writing a letter to describe a problem**

Dear Abby letters are very popular in American newspapers. An anonymous writer sends a letter to Abby asking her for suggestions to a problem.

Write Abby a short letter describing a problem you are having at school or work with an annoying classmate or coworker. (You may use an example from the list you brainstormed with your group.) Write clearly and legibly because you are going to send this letter to a classmate who will pretend he/she is Abby.

Your teacher will give everyone an identification number that you will write on your letter. No one will know your number but you. Your letter will be anonymous, just like *Dear Abby* letters in newspapers.

EXAMPLE:

Dear Abby:

In my English class, we work in teams. Every day we have certain jobs we are supposed to do as a team. One of our responsibilities is to call if we are going to be absent. If someone in the team doesn't call, our team won't get points for that day. I really want to get the points, because at the end of the month the team with the most points gets the Team of the Month award. One of the team members never calls when he is absent. It really bothers me that he doesn't think about how that affects us. What should I do?

Sincerely,

Frustrated Francis

PRACTICE: **Writing a solution to a problem**

Read the letter you received from an anonymous classmate. Write a letter back to your classmate in which you suggest a solution to his or her problem.

Use at least one of the suggestions you read in the article in your letter of advice. Use the grammar and expressions you learned in this chapter to express your advice in a correct and polite manner.

Write clearly and legibly.

EXAMPLE:

Dear Frustrated Francis:

If were you, I would talk to the student about why he's not calling. Maybe he doesn't understand the point system your teacher uses. Perhaps he doesn't know what to say when he calls and feels embarrassed. If that is the case, you ought to teach him what to say. Why don't you explain the rules of the class to him and encourage him to be a winner of the next Team of the Month award?

Sincerely,

Abby

When you have finished writing your letter of advice, answer these questions to help you revise and edit your own writing.

Revision Checklist

Circle *yes* or *no*.

1. Did you give your classmate one or two solutions to his/her problem?   YES   NO

2. Did you use at least one suggestion from the article?   YES   NO
   Which suggestion did you use?

   _____

3. Did you use words such as **should**, **ought to**, or **had better** to give advice?   YES   NO

4. Are all the verbs in the correct tense?   YES   NO
   (Check each verb and make corrections if necessary.)

5. Are all the words spelled correctly?   YES   NO
   (If you're not sure, use a dictionary to check the spelling.)

6. Does every sentence begin with a capital letter?   YES   NO

7. Does every sentence end with a period?   YES   NO

8. Is your writing neat and legible?   YES   NO
   (If you circled *no*, rewrite the letter neatly and legibly.)

Using math to communicate

PREPARATION: **Thinking about the survey questions**

A "pet peeve" is something that really annoys or bothers you.

1. What is your pet peeve when you go to a movie? When you go shopping? When you're taking public transportation?

_____

_____

_____

2. Does someone in your family do something that really bothers you?

_____

_____

_____

PRACTICE: **Interpreting a bar graph**

In May 1996 the Norelco Company surveyed 330 office workers on their pet peeves in the office. According to the survey, the office workers' complaints were divided into two categories: environmental and social.

NORELCO CLEARING THE AIR SURVEY	NORELCO CLEARING THE AIR SURVEY
Top 5 Environmental "Pet Peeves" in the Workplace	**Top 5 Social "Pet Peeves" in the Workplace**
Room Temperature — 56%	Coworker's Irritating Habits — 36%
Noise — 37%	Office Gossip — 29%
Odors — 25%	Overbearing/Difficult Boss — 25%
Uncomfortable/Cramped Offices — 23%	Foul Language — 18%
Messy Workstations/Common Areas — 22%	Speakerphones — 12%
Source: Norelco Consumer Products Company's Clean Air Systems	Source: Norelco Consumer Products Company's Clean Air Systems

In your group of four, look at the bar graph that summarizes the survey and answer these questions.

1. What was the biggest complaint about the office environment? What was the second biggest complaint? _____

   _____

   _____

2. What was the biggest complaint about what happens socially in the office? What was the second biggest social pet peeve? _____

   _____

   _____

PRACTICE: **Changing percents to whole numbers**

56% of the 330 people Norelco surveyed said room temperature bothered them the most.

How many people is that? Do you know how to figure this out?

56% of 330 people is _____

In math, **of** means **multiply** (or **times**) and **is** means **equals**. To multiply, change the percent (56%) to a decimal by moving the decimal point two places to the left:

56% = .56

Then multiply:

.56 X 330 = 184.8

To express a decimal as a whole number, **round off** (or eliminate) the decimal as follows:

- **round up** to the next number if the number after the decimal is 5 or above.

- **round down** to the number below if the number after the decimal is 4 or below.

The result of the Norelco survey, 184.8, can be rounded off to 185. This means that 185 people said that room temperature bothered them the most.

Can you do it? How many people had these complaints? To find out, change the percentages in the rest of the bar graph to whole numbers. Follow the example above.

1. Room temperature   <u>185</u>

2. Noise   _____

3. Odors   _____

4. Uncomfortable spaces   _____

5. Messy workstations   _____

6. Coworker's irritating habits   _____

7. Office gossip   _____

8. Overbearing boss   _____

9. Foul language   _____

10. Speakerphones   _____

EVALUATION: **Calculating percentages and drawing bar graphs**

What pet peeves do your classmates have?

- Count the number of people in your group who say that a problem listed in the chart is one of their pet peeves.

- Group recorders: Write your group's totals on the board.

- Tally the pet peeves of the whole class.

- Calculate the percentages of students who said that a problem listed in the chart is one of their pet peeves.

- Draw a bar graph like Norelco's.

Look at the example on the next page to help you do the activity.

EXAMPLE:

■ There are 35 students in class X. Seventeen of these students said that room temperature was their pet peeve.

■ To express the number as a percentage, divide the number of students who named room temperature as their pet peeve by the total number of students in the class:

$17 \div 35 = .49$

■ To express this decimal as a percentage, move the decimal point two places to the right:

49% of the class said room temperature was their pet peeve.

	GROUP 1	GROUP 2	GROUP 3	GROUP 4	GROUP 5	GROUP 6	TOTAL
room temperature							
noise							
odors							
uncomfortable							
space							
messy areas							

TOTAL # OF _____ STUDENTS

classmates							
gossip							
hard teacher							
speaking language other than English							
other							

TOTAL # OF _____ STUDENTS

 # Check it!

Put a checkmark next to each activity you accomplished in this chapter.

ACADEMIC SKILLS CHECKLIST

Did you . . .

_____ write new vocabulary words in a notebook?

_____ write new grammar words in a notebook?

_____ figure out the meaning of words by using contextual clues?

_____ use resources, such as a dictionary or a thesaurus, inside the classroom?

_____ interpret and communicate information from the article?

_____ paraphrase a suggestion from the article?

_____ interpret and explain a bar graph?

_____ use **should, ought to,** or **had better** to give advice?

_____ use **would rather** to express your preferences?

_____ write a letter giving someone solutions to a problem?

_____ use the Internet to get more information about the topic?

WORK SKILLS CHECKLIST

Did you . . .

_____ work effectively in your team?

_____ teach a classmate something new? What did you teach? _____

_____ use math to figure out the bar graph?

_____ survey your classmates to find out about complaints in your classroom?
What was the biggest complaint about your classroom? _____

_____ draw a bar graph to express the percentages of students with specific
complaints in your classroom?

_____ use appropriate language to give advice politely? What is one expression
you used? _____

Chapter 8

Handling Criticism

OBJECTIVES

By the end of this chapter, you will be able to:

- Teach classmates information you acquired from an article.

- Suggest positive ways to handle criticism.

- Use key words to paraphrase an article.

- Explain a problem, find the best solution to it, and explain the consequences of the solution you chose.

- Write a paragraph using information from a flowchart.

- Revise and edit your own and a classmate's paragraph.

- Ask and answer negative questions.

- Use appropriate language to offer and accept an apology.

To be successful at school and at work, you need to have certain basic skills and qualities. In this chapter, you will focus on the following skills and qualities:

1. Analyzing and interpreting information

2. Using contextual clues to figure out definitions

3. Using a problem-solving flowchart to help solve a problem

4. Monitoring and correcting pronunciation

Talk about it!

Think about a situation in which you or someone you know was criticized. Jot down some notes to answer these questions. Then discuss them with the class.

1. What was the reason for the criticism?

2. How did you (or the person being criticized) react? What did you, he, or she do?

3. Did the problem get resolved?

Take it down!

Your teacher will dictate a paragraph that covers the content and grammar in this chapter. First, write what you hear. Then check it by using the Dictation Revision Form on the back inside cover.

_____

_____

_____

_____

 # Read about it!

PREPARATION: **Brainstorming ideas for handling a difficult situation**

No one likes getting criticism, but it can help us do things better. What is the best way to handle criticism?

Brainstorm. In a group of four students, brainstorm good ways to react when you are criticized.

STUDENT 1:

On a sheet of blank paper, write one thing that is important for a person to think, say, or do when he or she is criticized. When the teacher gives the signal, pass the paper to Student 2.

STUDENT 2:

Write another thing that is important for a person to think, say, or do when he or she is criticized. When the teacher gives the signal, pass the paper to Student 3, who will do the same before passing the list of ideas to Student 4.

ALL STUDENTS:

Everyone in the group must write at least one idea about what a person should do or say when he or she receives criticism.

PRACTICE: **Interpreting and communicating information**

A. Read the article. Remain in your group of four students.

STUDENTS 1 AND 2:

Read and discuss steps 1–5 of the article.

STUDENTS 3 AND 4:

Read and discuss steps 6–10 of the article.

Ten Steps for Handling Criticism

1 Remain calm!
The easiest thing to do is get upset. Instead, have an open mind. The person criticizing you may have something worthwhile to say.

2 Don't take it personally.
Keep your self-confidence. You are being criticized for something you *did*, not something you *are*.

3 Listen!
Often we use the time someone else is talking to figure out what our response is going to be. Instead, give your full attention to what is being said.

4 Make sure you understand.
In your own words, repeat what the person has said to you. Make sure you've got it right.

5 Ask for time to think about it.
Don't respond right away unless you're forced to. Tell the person you need time to take this all in.

6 Compare what is being said with what you know about yourself.
Sit down in a quiet place and think about what the person said. Is it factually correct? Could it be true? Why are you feeling so upset about this? Sometimes the truth hurts.

7 Share the criticism.
Talk with someone who knows you well, and ask that person what he or she thinks. That's what friends are for. Share the criticism with a person you really trust. Ask for your friend's honest opinion.

8 Decide whether you agree with the criticism.
This is up to you and nobody else. All of us can improve; maybe the person has a point. But don't beat yourself up either. Maybe the person doesn't have a point.

9 Decide what action you're going to take.
If you agree with the criticism, what should you do? What might you change? Think in terms of action.

10 Respond to the criticizer.
This is sometimes the hardest thing of all. Figure out what you're going to say and then say it. Tell the criticizer what you've decided, what steps you've taken, and what you're going to do now. Make sure you stay calm.

Source: TQS 4.4: Handling Conflict or Criticism in a Team Handling Criticism, Modified 1/10/97 http://iasec.fwsd.wednet.edu/ tqs/private/unit04/les4402.htm

B. Interpret the article. Work with your classmates to interpret each section of the article.

STUDENTS 1 AND 2

1. Find the following words in steps 1–5 of the article. Then write a synonym or brief definition of each word. Use a dictionary if necessary.

    a. remain: _____

    b. upset: _____

    c. instead: _____

    d. figure out: _____

2. How can you show a person who is criticizing you that you understand what he or she is saying? _____

    _____

    _____

    _____

3. What do we sometimes do while a person is criticizing us? What should we do instead? _____

    _____

    _____

4. At the beginning of this chapter you described a situation in which you or someone you know was criticized. Explain the reason for the criticism and how you (or the person who was criticized) reacted. Did you (or he/she) follow any of the steps you read about in the article? Which one(s)? _____

    _____

    _____

    _____

5. Reread steps 1–5. With a highlighter pen, highlight the key words in each step. A **key word** expresses the main idea of a statement or paragraph.

1. Find the following words in steps 6-10 of the article. Then write a synonym or brief definition of each word. Use a dictionary if necessary.

   a. share: _____

   b. trust: _____

   c. whether: _____

   d. beat yourself up: _____

2. If someone criticizes you, whom should you tell about the criticism? Whom would you tell? _____

   _____

   _____

   _____

3. In one of the steps it is suggested that you go to a quiet place. In your own words, what should you do during this quiet time? _____

   _____

   _____

   _____

   _____

4. At the beginning of this chapter you described a situation in which you or someone you know was criticized. Explain the reason for the criticism and how you (or the person who was criticized) reacted. Did you (or she/he) follow any of the steps you read about in the article? Which one(s)? _____

   _____

   _____

   _____

5. Reread steps 6-10. With a highlighter pen, highlight the key words in each step. A **key word** expresses the main idea of a statement or paragraph.

PRACTICE: **Using key words to paraphrase**

When you **paraphrase** an article or reading passage, you explain its most important points in your own words. First, copy the key words you highlighted. Then, looking only at these words and not the article, write a paraphrase of the steps for handling criticism. Next, read your paraphrase to another student in your group and listen to his or her paraphrase of the article. Be sure to ask your partner questions if any of the steps he or she paraphrased is not clear.

EVALUATION: **Understanding your teammates**

Demonstrate that you understood your teammates by writing down three of the steps for handling criticism that they paraphrased. Do not look at the article or write any of the steps you were responsible for paraphrasing. Your teacher will ask certain students to write the steps they learned from their teammates on the board.

 O N L I N E !

NOTE

If you don't have a computer or cannot get on the Internet at home, you can:

1. Go to a public library near your home or school. Libraries usually have free Internet access.

2. Find out if you can get on the Internet at your school. Schools often have Internet access.

3. Ask a friend if you can use his or her computer to get on the Internet.

A. **Search.** For more advice about how to handle criticism, look up these addresses or search on your own:

■ Handling criticism at work:
http://goodhousekeeping.com/gh/advice/47brotb4.htm

■ Handling conflict or criticism in a team:
http://iasec.fwsd.wednet.edu/tqs/private/unit04/les4402.htm

■ Six keys to successfully handling criticism:
http://www.salesdoctors.com/mindrobics/sim13.htm

B. **Report.** After you find the addresses, tell your classmates or write a brief paragraph about ways to handle criticism.

Practical grammar: Negative question

USAGE

Use negative questions in these situations:

■ To show surprise or doubt:

> **Didn't** you hear the phone? It rang six times.
> **Aren't** you going to answer it?

■ When you expect the listener to agree with you:

> You worked on that report all night! **Aren't** you tired?
> **Why don't** you go home early and get some rest?

■ In an exclamation:

> **Isn't** that computer fast!

FORM

Notice the word order of negative questions.

QUESTION	HELPING VERB	SUBJECT	VERB	
	Didn't	you	hear	the phone?
Why	didn't	you	answer	the phone?
	Aren't	you	going	to answer it?
	Doesn't	he	work	downtown?
Why	won't	he	work	overtime?
	Weren't	you		late yesterday?

Can you do it? With a partner, read the following questions. Write **C** if the question is correctly written, **I** if it is incorrectly written. If a question is incorrectly written, discuss the reason with your partner and correct it.

1. _____ Why you don't help me clean up this area?

2. _____ Why doesn't he gives us more time to finish this report?

3. _____ Why won't they attend the staff meeting?

4. _____ Why the secretary didn't leave the message on my desk?

5. _____ Why don't you file those invoices before you leave?

A. Asking negative questions.

STUDENT 1: Read each sentence and ask your partner a negative question with **why**.

STUDENT 2: Answer each question with a complete sentence.

EXAMPLE: STUDENT 1:   Stella didn't go to work today.
                       Why didn't Stella go to work today?

             STUDENT 2:   She didn't go because she has the flu.

1. Abraham can't come to the meeting.
   Why _____

   _____

2. The supervisor wasn't at work today.
   Why _____

   _____

3. The employee didn't get a promotion.
   Why _____

   _____

4. Richard's report isn't ready yet.
   Why _____

   _____

5. Carlos won't be in class tomorrow.
   Why _____

   _____

Now switch roles: Student 2, ask the questions. Student 1, answer the questions.

6. The clerical workers can't find the patients' folders.
   Why _____

   _____

7. Anita shouldn't turn her assignment in late.
   Why _____

   _____

8. The engineers aren't going to make the deadline.

    Why _____

    _____

9. The assemblers on the third shift don't want to work overtime.

    Why _____

    _____

    _____

10. The managers weren't in a very good mood yesterday.

    Why _____

    _____

Offering and accepting apologies

In many situations in your daily life, you will have to deal with criticism. At school and at work you may at times make mistakes, forget something, or do the wrong thing. Your friends and coworkers might criticize you for something you have done improperly or a mistake you have made. It's important to have a positive attitude when you are criticized, to listen carefully to the comments, and learn from your mistakes. Apologize and accept the criticism graciously if you agree that you have, in fact, done something wrong. Use these expressions for offering an apology:

Please accept my apology.	Please forgive me.
It won't happen again.	I'm sorry.
I apologize.	

Sometimes you will be the person who has a criticism to make. If you have criticized a friend or coworker and that person has apologized to you, accept the apology graciously. Here are some expressions for accepting an apology:

These things happen.	I can show you how to do it
We all make mistakes.	right the next time.
You're only human.	

Say it! Use these expressions to offer and accept apologies graciously as you role play the situations in Exercise B.

B. Offering and accepting apologies. With a partner, role-play, offering and accepting apologies in the situations shown in each illustration. Use negative questions, as in the example, but substitute different apologies and acceptances for the sentences in bold type and make up your own ending. Refer to **How To Say It** on page 137 for substitions you can use.

STUDENT 1: Didn't you add up my bill wrong?

STUDENT 2: Umm, I think you're right. **Please accept my apology.**

STUDENT 1: Oh well. **These things happen.**

STUDENT 2: I'll fix it and be right back.

EXAMPLE: You added up my bill wrong.

1. "You came back late from lunch."

2. "You were late for the meeting."

3. "You forgot to tighten the lever."

4. "You filed the names spelled with GO before the names with GE."

5. "You took off on Friday without permission."

6. Make up a situation of your own in which one person is criticizing another.

◈ Write it down!

Figuring out a problem

Melissa Patterson is a clerical worker in a busy doctor's office and Sara Jenkins is her supervisor. Get into teams of five to read their conversation and figure out the problem and what's causing it. First, two team members will role-play Melissa's and Sara's conversation. Remember the basic pronunciation rules.

■ Speak slowly.

■ Emphasize the stressed syllables of the words.

■ Your voice should go down at the end of a sentence.

SJ: Melissa, I called you into my office to talk about your job performance. How long have you been working with us now?

MP: I've been here for about three months. Is there something wrong?

SJ: First of all, I commend you on your ability to talk to the patients and make them feel comfortable.

MP: Thank you for saying so.

SJ: However, things are not running smoothly in the office. Haven't you noticed the problems we've been having with patients' folders?

MP: No, not really. Aren't the folders neat? Didn't I type the names the way you asked me to?

SJ: Well, neatness isn't the issue here. Your coworkers are having trouble finding patients' folders. I've seen patients waiting quite a long time while the front desk clerk goes through the files looking for their folders.

MP: Why didn't the other clerks say something to me directly if they couldn't find something?

SJ: It's not just the other workers who are frustrated. Last week I was looking for an invoice in Doug Pearson's folder and it wasn't there. I finally found it in another patient's folder.

Discuss the situation in your teams. Why do you think Melissa's coworkers are frustrated? Why do you think her supervisor is upset with her? What is the problem? What things might be causing the problem? Each person on the team will take one of the following jobs:

LEADER: Lead the discussion and make sure everyone speaks. Use the expressions on page 151 to encourage everyone to participate.

TIMEKEEPER: Watch the clock and make sure your team stays within the time your teacher gives you. Don't let anyone talk for too long.

RECORDER: Write your team's answers to the questions.

GRAMMAR COP: Make sure everyone uses grammar correctly in speaking and in writing.

REPORTER: Report your team's answers back to the whole class.

The problem: _____

_____

_____

Causes of the problem: _____

_____

_____

PRACTICE: Solving a problem

Now that you have figured out what the problem is and what is causing it, work with your teammates to come up with some solutions. Use the Problem/Solutions/Consequences flowchart to do this.

First, each team member will fill out his or her chart individually. Then everyone will work together to fill out one chart for the team. The recorder will write out the team chart. The grammar cop will check it for spelling, punctuation, and grammar. Follow these steps to complete the chart:

■ Decide what options Melissa has. What can she do to respond to her supervisor's criticism? Write each option on the chart.

■ Think about and discuss the consequences – good or bad – of each option. Write each consequence on the chart.

■ As a team, decide on the solution that you all agree is the best one. Give your reasons for deciding on that option. Write what Melissa should do and the reasons why on the chart.

Problem/Solutions/Consequences

Options: What can Melissa do to solve the problem?

What can Melissa do? Option #1

Consequences

Good _____

_____

Bad _____

What can Melissa do? Option #2

Consequences

Good _____

_____

Bad _____

What can Melissa do? Option #3

Consequences

Good _____

_____

Bad _____

What do you think Melissa should do?

_____

_____

Why?

_____

_____

REPORTERS: Tell the whole class which action your team decided was best for Melissa and explain why.

EVALUATION: **Monitor and correct your work**

At work there are occasions when your supervisor might ask you to evaluate your job performance or the performance of a coworker. Evaluate the members of your team (including yourself) according to the questions in the chart.

2 points = very good   1 point = average   0 points = needs improvement

	STUDENT 1	STUDENT 2	STUDENT 3	STUDENT 4	STUDENT 5
Did student give a solution?					
Did student explain consequences of the solution?					
Did student help other students on the team?					
Did student do his or her job?					

1. How well did your team score? What do you need to pay more attention to as a team the next time you do an activity like this one?

2. How did the score you gave yourself compare with the one your teammates gave you? What do you need to pay more attention to as an individual the next time you do an activity like this one?

PRACTICE: **Writing a paragraph**

Use your completed Problem/Solutions/Consequences flowchart to write a paragraph about Melissa's problem and how she could have handled it.

After you complete your paragraph, give it to a classmate to read. Your classmate will evaluate your paragraph by completing this revision checklist. Make changes in your paragraph if you agree with your classmate's suggestions.

Classmate Revision Checklist

WRITER'S NAME: _____

CHECKER'S NAME: _____

Circle *yes* or *no*.

1. Is the writing neat and legible?   YES   NO
   (If you circled *no*, ask the writer to rewrite it.)

2. Does everything make sense?   YES   NO
   (If you circled *no*, ask the writer to explain the
   part that is confusing. Then help the writer revise it.)

3. Did the writer suggest an option for Melissa to   YES   NO
   handle the problem and explain the consequence
   of taking this action?
   (If you circled *no*, help the writer to come up with
   at least one option and consequence. Then ask the
   writer to describe them in writing.)

4. Check all the verbs. Are they in the correct tense?   YES   NO
   (If you circled *no*, help the writer correct them.)

5. Are all the words spelled correctly?   YES   NO
   (If you circled *no*, make corrections. If you are
   unsure of the spelling, use a dictionary.)

6. Are the periods and commas in the correct places?   YES   NO
   (If you circled *no*, help the writer correct the punctuation.)

7. Is there anything you especially liked about   YES   NO
   this paragraph? What did you like? _____

   _____

 # Check it!

Put a checkmark next to each activity you accomplished in this chapter.

ACADEMIC SKILLS CHECKLIST

Did you . . .

_____ write new vocabulary words in a notebook?

_____ write new grammar rules in a notebook?

_____ interpret and communicate information from the article?

_____ use key words to paraphrase ideas in the article? What is one idea you paraphrased? _____

_____

_____ use resources, such as a dictionary or a thesaurus, inside the classroom?

_____ write a paragraph describing the solution to a problem and the consequences of that solution?

_____ evaluate a classmate's paragraph using the revision checklist?

_____ ask and answer negative questions correctly?

_____ use the Internet to find more information on the topic?

WORK SKILLS CHECKLIST

Did you . . .

_____ work effectively in your team?

_____ do the job that was assigned to you? What was your job?
_____

_____ teach someone something? What did you teach? _____

_____

_____ organize and maintain information on a flowchart?

_____ solve a problem? What was the problem? _____

_____

_____ negotiate with your classmates to decide together on the best solution? What was the solution? _____

_____

_____ correct a classmate's pronunciation?

_____ assess your own and your teammates' performance?

_____ use appropriate expressions to offer and accept apologies? What is one expression you used? _____

Chapter 9

Having a Positive Attitude

By the end of this chapter, you will be able to:

■ Teach classmates information you acquired from an article.

■ Paraphrase parts of an article.

■ Describe specific characteristics of a positive attitude.

■ Explain the connection between work performance and attitude.

■ Suggest ways to deal with classmates or coworkers who have negative attitudes.

■ Write a letter of appreciation in business or personal letter format.

■ Revise your own and a classmate's letter.

■ Demonstrate your knowledge of subject-verb agreement.

■ Use appropriate language to bring people into the conversation.

To be successful at school and at work, you need to have certain basic skills and qualities. In this chapter, you will focus on the following skills and qualities:

- Analyzing and interpreting information

- Building self-esteem

- Writing business letters

- Finding solutions in negative situations

Talk about it!

1. What does having a positive attitude mean? Do you think you have a positive attitude? Why or why not?

2. Have you been with a classmate, coworker, or family member who had a negative attitude? How did that person's attitude influence you?

Take it down!

Your teacher will dictate a paragraph that covers the content and the grammar in this chapter. First, write what you hear. Then check it by using the Dictation Revision Form on the back inside cover.

_____

_____

_____

_____

_____

◈ Read about it!

PREPARATION: **Describing positive and negative traits**

A. What trait (characteristic) should all job seekers have? With a partner, read the want ads. Then answer the questions together.

a.

☎

RECEPTIONIST
Oppty. for person to join small software company. Person must have pleasant phone voice and a positive attitude.

b.

AUTOMOTIVE TECHNICIAN

Lube technician. Full-time position. Great entry-level position for a quality-oriented person with the right attitude.

c.

GENERAL OFFICE
We need 5 great people with excellent attitude. For office work, receptionist, management trainee, counter sales, and outside sales.

d.

NURSING
CNA A.M. and nights avl. Need to be highly motivated, compassionate, care deeply for the elderly, and have a positive attitude.

1. What jobs are advertised? _____

_____

2. What quality do all four jobs require? _____

_____

3. How would you describe a person who has that quality?

_____

_____

4. Do you have that quality? How do you demonstrate that quality?

_____

_____

B. How does a person who has a good attitude behave? Having a good attitude will help you get along well with your coworkers, boss, classmates, and family. Many companies require not only the necessary skills to do the job, but a good attitude as well. With your classmates, read about how people with good (and bad) attitudes behave. Later in this chapter you will practice being positive. Form groups of three, and give each student a number from 1 to 3.

STUDENT 1: Read aloud the traits of people with a positive attitude.

STUDENT 2: Read aloud the traits of people with a negative attitude.

STUDENT 3: If anyone in your group doesn't understand a word, look it up in the dictionary and explain the definition.

PEOPLE WITH A POSITIVE ATTITUDE	PEOPLE WITH A NEGATIVE ATTITUDE
■ respect other people's opinions	■ expect other people to share their opinions
■ work well in a team	■ don't work well with others
■ are considerate	■ think mostly of themselves
■ rarely criticize others	■ are critical of others
■ smile often	■ rarely smile
■ don't make excuses	■ often make excuses
■ accept responsibility for their mistakes	■ blame others for their mistakes
■ are willing to change their ideas	■ are unwilling to change their ideas
■ can see another person's point of view	■ can't see another person's point of view
■ seldom complain	■ complain about everything

C. How can you help build a positive attitude? Write the answers to the following questions on your own paper. Then share your answers to question 3 with your group and the whole class.

1. What are three of your positive traits?

2. What are two of your negative traits?

3. What can you do if someone in your class or at your job has a negative attitude?

A. Read the article. First read the article to yourself. Then answer these focus questions.

1. There are nine words that have negative connotations in the first paragraph. Write them down.

   _____

   _____

2. There are five numbered items in the article. What does the information in numbers 1-5 refer to?

   _____

   _____

Fight Negative Work Attitudes

Don't be negative. A sense of injustice, of being treated unfairly, is the most common cause of workplace negativity, "a contagious disease that cripples employee morale and bleeds profit," said Sheila Ruth, a professor at Southern Illinois University at Edwardsville.

Ruth, who specializes in managing negative behavior in the workplace, reports that at some work sites, "you can feel the negativity crackling in the walls."

The results often are an increase in employee mistakes, accidents, absenteeism, theft, high turnover, low morale, and angry customers–not a pretty picture.

Though a negative workplace is management's problem, there are some things employees can do to combat its toxic effects, according to Ruth:

❶ Decide if you want to continue working there.

❷ Keep away from employees who constantly complain.

❸ Don't let the negativity become a part of your personality.

❹ Don't feed the rumor mill.

❺ Don't let the negativity spill over to your private life.

And be proactive in encouraging your company to clean up some of the toxic aspects of work that pollute the air at the office or plant.

Source: Carol Kleiman, *Chicago Tribune*, reprinted in the *San Diego Union-Tribune*, 9/8/96

Bringing other people into a conversation

At school or at work, in meetings or conferences, there may be people who are afraid or embarrassed to give their opinions. They probably would like to share their ideas or make a point but they don't know how to join in the conversation. Here are common expressions you may use to draw other people into a conversation:

> What do you think, (person's name)?
> What's your opinion, (person's name)?
> Do you agree with us, (person's name)?
> How do you feel about this, (person's name)?

Say it! Use these expressions to encourage your teammates to participate as you work together to interpret the article.

B. Interpret the article. In a group of four students, number 1–4. Work with your classmates to interpret the article.

STUDENTS 1 AND 2

1. The article uses a lot of interesting vocabulary to describe things. For example, it says that negativity:

   ■ is a contagious disease

   ■ cripples employee morale

   ■ bleeds profit

   a. Is it really a disease? _____

   b. Can it really cripple people? _____

   c. Can it really make something bleed? _____

   d. What do those three definitions of negativity make you think of?

   _____

2. Why does the author use those kinds of words to describe negativity?

   _____

1. What problems do negative attitudes cause in the workplace?

_____

2. When there is too much negativity in the workplace, who should make major changes? _____

C. Teach each other. Share the information you learned with each other.

STUDENT 1: Teach Student 3. Then switch roles.
STUDENT 2: Teach Student 4. Then switch roles.

PRACTICE: **Paraphrasing the article**

When you **paraphrase** the ideas in an article, you explain them in your own words. According to the article, employees can take action if they are working around negative people. Reread the five suggestions. Then, working with your teammates, take turns paraphrasing them and give an example of each one.

EVALUATION: **Understanding your teammates**

Demonstrate that you understood your teammates by writing down three of the suggestions for handling workplace negativity that they paraphrased. Do not look back at the article or write any of the suggestions that you paraphrased. Your teacher will ask certain students to write the suggestions they learned from their teammates on the board.

 O N L I N E !

NOTE

If you don't have a computer or cannot get on the Internet at home, you can:

1. Go to a public library near your home or school. Libraries usually have free Internet access.

2. Find out if you can get on the Internet at your school. Schools often have Internet access.

3. Ask a friend if you can use his or her computer to get on the Internet.

A. Search. For more dealing with negative attitudes, look up these addresses on the Internet or search on your own:

- Attitude:
  http://www.kcstar.com/library/library.htm
  click Library 97; type author Richelle Tremaine

- Break the bad attitude habit:
  http://www.shrm.org/hrmagazine/articles/0797tool.htm

B. Report. After you find the addresses, tell your classmates or write a brief paragraph about ways to deal with negative attitudes.

Remaining positive in negative situations

Now that you have thought about the subject and read the article, see if you can apply what you learned. With a partner, role play the following situations. One person will behave negatively; the other will maintain a good attitude. Refer to Activity B on page 149 for ideas about how positive people react.

■ A customer placed his order but you didn't understand and had to ask him several times to repeat it. Later, another employee said sarcastically, "How did you get hired?" What could you do or say to remain positive?

■ You work at a busy furniture store. Your boss said you should be more friendly to the customers. What could you do or say to be positive about your boss's comment?

■ You were absent from work because you had a cold. A coworker said, "Since you weren't here yesterday I had to do your job and mine too." How might you maintain a good attitude while responding to your coworker's remark?

EVALUATION: **Monitor and correct your work**

Role-play your situations in front of the class. Vote to decide who had the most positive attitude.

 Write it up!

PREPARATION: **Describing the purpose and audience of business letters**

Whenever you write a letter or an essay, it's important to think about your purpose or reason for writing and who the person or people you are writing to will be.

A. Purpose. In a group of four students, write down as many examples as you can of when you may need to write a business letter.

_____

_____

_____

_____

B. Purpose and audience. The situations below would all require a business letter. Take turns reading each situation in your group. Then write the purpose for each letter and who the audience would be.

1. Your sink has been leaking for three days and you already told the landlord twice.

   Purpose: _____ Audience: _____

2. You would like to get more information about a computer you saw in a magazine.

   Purpose: _____ Audience: _____

3. You ordered three boxes of paper but you received only two.

   Purpose: _____ Audience: _____

4. A good friend asked you to write a letter recommending him for a job.

   Purpose: _____ Audience: _____

5. You are applying for a job. You have already filled out the application and a résumé.

   Purpose: _____ Audience: _____

6. You just had an interview and you want to let the interviewer know you appreciate his or her time.

   Purpose: _____ Audience: _____

7. You invited a speaker by phone to come to your class to give a talk. Now you want to confirm that he or she will come to the class.

   Purpose: _____ Audience: _____

8. The people in your office are having a pot-luck supper. They want to invite the supervisor's wife to come to the party.

   Purpose: _____ Audience: _____

◆ Practical grammar: Subject-verb agreement

BASIC SUBJECT-VERB AGREEMENT

When you speak or write, it's important to make the subject and the verb of every sentence agree, because this helps the listener or reader understand exactly what you are talking about. In most cases, singular subjects require singular verbs. Plural subjects require plural verbs.

> My uncle works in a bank.
> (The subject **uncle** is singular; the verb **works** is singular.)
>
> The manual on how to use that computer is in the drawer.
> (The subject **manual** is singular; the verb **is** is singular.)
>
> The suggestions she gave were very important to her supervisor.
> (The subject **suggestions** is plural; the verb **were** is plural.)

Can you do it? Underline the subject of each sentence below. If the subject is singular, write **S** above it. If the subject is plural, write **P** above it. Then circle the correct verb.

1. The technician (is/are) repairing the copier.

2. Teresa and Raymond (was/were) the supervisors for the graveyard shift.

3. The number of promotions (increase/increases) every year at that growing company.

4. The insurance forms (have/has) changed since last year.

5. Information you write on your application (is/are) confidential.

COMMON ERRORS MADE IN SUBJECT-VERB AGREEMENT

Some nouns that end in -s are singular. They take singular verbs, and the pronoun **it**, not **they**, is used to refer to them:

- United States

    The United States is an enormous country. **It stretches** from the Atlantic to the Pacific Ocean.

■ news

> The **news is** essential for everyone to know.
> Do you prefer to watch **it** on TV or read **it** in the newspaper?

■ classes or fields of study that end in **-ics**

> **Mathematics is** a required course. **It is** one of my favorite classes.

■ expressions of time, money, and distance

> **Ten hours** of work a day **is** the maximum you should do.
> Do you think **four hundred dollars** a week **is** a good
>   salary for that job?
> **Fifty miles is** a long distance to travel to work every day.

Can you do it? Underline the noun that ends in **-s.** Circle the verb.

1. Physics is fascinating to some people.

2. The United States has a diverse population.

3. Fifty minutes is the usual time for a class at this school.

4. The news about the strike was unexpected.

5. Ten hours of sleep is probably too much for an adult.

AGREEMENT WITH INDEFINITE PRONOUNS

When you want to talk about a person, place, or thing that isn't specifically identified, use an indefinite pronoun.

INDEFINITE PRONOUNS USED WITH SINGULAR VERBS:

anybody	everybody	nobody	somebody
anyone	everyone	no one	someone
anything	everything	nothing	something
either	neither	much	

Everyone is taking **his** or **her** family to the staff party.
Anybody who **wants** time off must ask **his** or **her** supervisor.

INDEFINITE PRONOUNS USED WITH PLURAL VERBS:

both   many

few   others

Both of the technicians **were** proud of **their** bonuses.
Few employees **eat** during **their** designated lunch breaks.

INDEFINITE PRONOUNS USED WITH SINGULAR OR PLURAL VERBS:

all   most

any   none

more   some

Most of **those computers** are expensive.
(count noun + plural verb)

Most of **that hardware** is expensive.
(noncount noun + singular verb)

When using indefinite pronouns, remember:

■ They must agree in number with the verb.

   Everyone in that class **needs** to buy a disk.
   Many already **have** a supply of disks.

■ They must agree in number and gender with the noun/pronoun they refer to.

   Everyone has **his** or **her** own locker.

Can you do it? Underline the indefinite pronoun. Circle the verb. Put a box around the noun/pronoun that refers to the indefinite pronoun.

1. Anybody who goes to the meeting must sign his or her own name on the list.

2. When it rains, someone always forgets his or her umbrella.

3. All of the employees must decide on their vacation schedule.

4. Nobody leaves the building until his or her test is turned in.

5. Everyone has to get along with his or her supervisor.

Complete each sentence in your own words. Use **is** or **are** in your answers.

EXAMPLE: His ideas <u>are interesting.</u>

1. Many of my _____

2. The United States _____

3. Everyone at the office party _____

4. Nobody at the office party _____

5. The news _____

6. Both _____

7. Neither _____

8. All _____

9. None _____

10. No one _____

EVALUATION: **Monitor and correct your work**

Exchange papers with a classmate. Check for subject-verb agreement. If you disagree with any of the answers, tell your partner and give a suggestion for changing it. (Refer to Chapter 4 for common expressions on giving suggestions.)

PRACTICE: **Writing a thank-you letter**

As you read in the article, one of the causes of workplace negativity is a sense of being treated unfairly. Whether in the workplace, in class, or elsewhere, people feel resentment when they work very hard and don't get recognized for it. When something bad has happened, we are quick to let people know about it. But how many of us take the time to show people that we appreciate their efforts, help, or contributions? A phone call, an e-mail message, or especially a brief note of thanks can do a great deal to improve morale in the workplace or classroom.

Write a letter of appreciation to a coworker or classmate. Think of a time that this person did something for you and explain how this action helped you. Your letter can be a personal note or a business thank-you letter.

Expressing gratitude

There are many ways to express gratitude in a thank-you letter. Use these expressions when you write your letters of appreciation.

> Thank you for your . . .
> I'm very grateful for . . .
> I want to express my gratitude for . . .
> I keep forgetting to thank you for . . .
> I appreciate your help.
> I look forward to working with you.
>   seeing you more in the future.
>   talking with you.

Say it! Use some of these expressions in the thank-you letter you write in the next activity.

A. Writing personal thank-you notes. A brief, personal letter is more noticed and appreciated than a store-bought card. Personal letters don't have to be typed. Remember these tips:

- Make your message simple and honest.

- Give a specific example of why you are appreciative.

Follow the format below when writing personal thank-you notes:

March 15, 1999 ———— date

salutation — Dear Janet,

Thank you for helping me in class last Wednesday. I was having a lot of trouble with the lesson because I was absent for two days. I really appreciate the time you took to explain the new vocabulary words to me. It makes a big difference having someone like you in class.

Your classmate, ———— closing

Lorena ———— signed name

B. Writing business thank-you letters. If you are writing a business thank-you letter, it is important to use the correct format. Here is the format that is typical of most business letters:

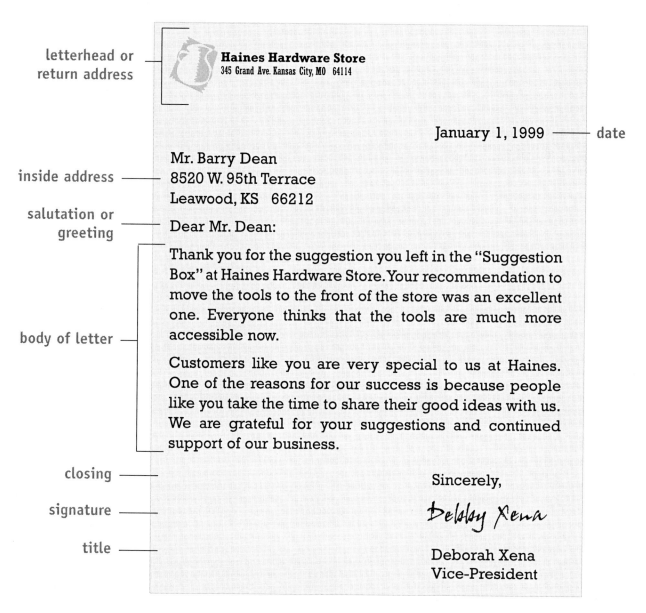

letterhead or return address

Haines Hardware Store
345 Grand Ave. Kansas City, MO 64114

January 1, 1999 — date

inside address

Mr. Barry Dean
8520 W. 95th Terrace
Leawood, KS 66212

salutation or greeting

Dear Mr. Dean:

body of letter

Thank you for the suggestion you left in the "Suggestion Box" at Haines Hardware Store. Your recommendation to move the tools to the front of the store was an excellent one. Everyone thinks that the tools are much more accessible now.

Customers like you are very special to us at Haines. One of the reasons for our success is because people like you take the time to share their good ideas with us. We are grateful for your suggestions and continued support of our business.

closing

Sincerely,

signature

Deborah Xena

title

Deborah Xena
Vice-President

EVALUATION: **Monitor and correct your work**

When you have finished writing your letter, find a partner and read it aloud to him or her. Remember the three basic pronunciation rules as you listen to your teacher read examples from the article.

■ **Speak slowly.**

Decide if you want to continue working there.

■ **Emphasize the stressed syllables of the words.**

Keep away from employees who constantly complain.

■ Let your voice go down at the end of a sentence.

Don't let the negativity become a part of your personality.

After you read your letter, give it to your classmate to check. Your classmate will evaluate the letter by completing this revision checklist.

Classmate Revision Checklist

WRITER'S NAME: _____

CHECKER'S NAME: _____

Circle *yes* or *no*.

1. Can you read the writer's handwriting?   YES   NO
   (If you circled *no*, ask the writer to rewrite it.)

2. Did the writer express gratitude for something   YES   NO
   specific? What expression did he or she use to
   show gratitude? _____

3. Check the format (for all letters).
   ■ Is there a date?   YES   NO
   ■ Is there a salutation?   YES   NO
   ■ What is the salutation? _____
   ■ Is there a closing?   YES   NO
   ■ What is the closing? _____
   ■ Did the person sign his or her name?   YES   NO

   For business letters:
   ■ Is there a return address?   YES   NO
   ■ Is there an inside address?   YES   NO
   ■ Is there a colon after the salutation?   YES   NO

4. Are all verbs in the correct tense?   YES   NO
   (If you circled *no*, help the writer correct them.)

5. Does each verb agree with its subject?   YES   NO
   (Refer to the *Practical Grammar* section in this chapter.
   If you circled *no*, help the writer make corrections.)

6. Are all the words spelled correctly?   YES   NO
   (If you circled *no*, help the writer make
   corrections. If you're not sure, use a dictionary.)

7. Does every sentence begin with a capital letter?   YES   NO

8. Does every sentence end with a period?   YES   NO

9. Do you think the writer is ready to send this letter?   YES   NO

Do you have a good attitude?

Rate yourself to see what your attitude score is!

4 = frequently
3 = sometimes
2 = rarely
1 = never

Do you . . .

_____ feel good about yourself?

_____ smile often?

_____ come to school prepared?

_____ greet your classmates or coworkers?

_____ make small talk with your classmates and coworkers?

_____ empathize with new students or coworkers?

_____ help your teacher without being asked?

_____ take an interest in your classmates or coworkers?

_____ try to make friends with your classmates or coworkers?

_____ do your homework?

_____ answer the phone when it rings?

_____ avoid complaining at work or school?

_____ try to help others?

_____ take responsibility for your actions?

_____ look at the good things?

_____ TOTAL

48–60 = You have a good attitude! Keep it up.

43–47 = Try to improve your attitude. Think about the changes you could make.

below 43 = What's wrong? Think about what you can do to make yourself and the people around you happier.

If you feel comfortable going over this assessment with someone else, do so. This will give you an opportunity to talk about your attitude and get some suggestions for how you might go about improving it.

 Check it!

Put a checkmark next to each activity you accomplished in this chapter.

ACADEMIC SKILLS CHECKLIST

Did you . . .

_____ write new vocabulary words in a notebook?

_____ write new grammar rules in a notebook?

_____ interpret and communicate information from the article?

_____ use resources, such as a dictionary or a thesaurus, inside the classroom?

_____ use the Internet to find more information about the topic?

_____ paraphrase some of the suggestions in the article and give examples?

_____ write a letter of appreciation?

_____ revise and edit a classmate's letter using the revision checklist?

_____ write sentences in which the subjects and verbs agreed?

WORK SKILLS CHECKLIST

Did you . . .

_____ work effectively in your group? What did you do to contribute to the success of your group?_____

_____ teach someone something? What did you teach?_____

_____ assess your positive and negative characteristics?

_____ learn some ideas from dealing with a coworker or classmate who has a negative attitude? What is one idea you learned? _____

_____ write a business or personal letter using the correct letter format?

_____ use appropriate expressions to express your gratitude? What is one expression you used? _____

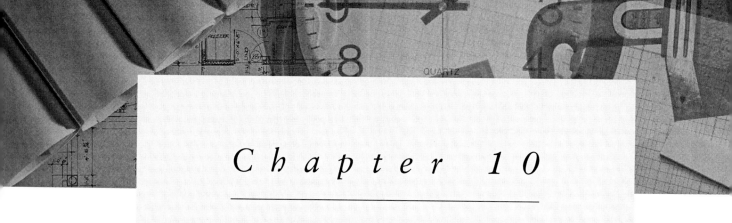

Chapter 10

Writing at Work

OBJECTIVES

By the end of this chapter, you will be able to:

■ Teach classmates information you acquired from an article.

■ Recognize common errors of content and grammar in a memo.

■ Recognize proper format in a memo.

■ Compose a memo, keeping in mind the two preceding objectives.

■ Revise and edit your own and a classmate's memo.

■ Describe when and how to use e-mail.

■ Identify when and how to use the passive voice.

■ Use appropriate language to give instructions.

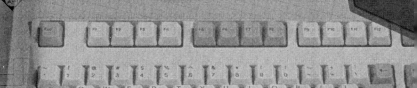

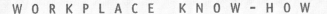

To be successful at school and at work, you need to have certain basic skills and qualities. In this chapter, you will focus on the following skills and qualities:

1. Interpreting and communicating information from an article

2. Using key words to paraphrase

3. Applying rules to answer questions about memo writing

4. Writing memos

5. Understanding technological systems

Talk about it!

1. What are the differences between memos, e-mail messages, and business letters?

2. Who writes memos and e-mails at work?

Take it down!

Your teacher will dictate a paragraph that covers the content and grammar in this chapter. First, write what you hear. Then check it by using the Dictation Revision Form on the back inside cover.

_____

_____

_____

_____

_____

◈ Read about it!

1. Read the title of the article on the facing page. Where are the original Ten Commandments and what do they describe? _____

   _____

   _____

   _____

   _____

   _____

2. What does the "Ten Commandments" mean in this title? _____

   _____

   _____

   _____

3. Have you ever written a memo? Where? Were there any "commandments" that you followed?_____

   _____

   _____

   _____

4. What are some other types of business correspondence besides memos? _____

   _____

   _____

   _____

PRACTICE: **Interpreting the main points**

A. Read the article. In teams of six, read the article. If you don't understand a word, try to guess its meaning or ask a teammate for the definition. Do not use your dictionary the first time you read. When you have finished reading the article, highlight the ten commandments.

These Ten Commandments Are for Writers of Memos

Like it or not, we are writing more than ever at work these days.

Faxes often require written responses. Computers, which many people thought would lead to the paperless office, have just made it easier to churn out reams of memos. Even e-mail, a chat in cyberspace, depends on the written – if not printed – word.

Much of what comes across our desks (and computer screens) is aimless, wordy, and boring. To help you look better in writing, follow these ten commandments:

1. **Be brief.** Whether you're sending an official memo or dashing off a quick e-mail message, start with a clear statement of why you're writing. ("We need extra help for our fall sales campaign, and I'd like permission to hire a temp.") Fit your memo on one page (about 250 words in e-mail), and make it simple to read. Short sentences (ten words or fewer) and paragraphs (no longer than four sentences) work best.

2. **Set the right tone.** Every office file includes memos written in anger or frustration. They leave a nasty paper trail. Write that irate note, if it's absolutely necessary, but delay sending it until you can make the tone more professional.

3. **Get personal.** To grab attention, address your reader directly with words like "we," "us," or "you." Impersonal words ("one") or phrasing ("staff should report all inquiries") are a turnoff.

4. **Weed out repetition.** Try not to repeat things you've already covered. And don't use many words when a few will do. Some of my favorite mouthfuls: "in connection with" (with), "in the event that" (if), and "the price is inclusive of" (the price includes).

5. **Use topic sentences.** Start each paragraph with a strong sentence summarizing what follows. ("This strategy can serve several purposes.") That way, someone who does not have time to read every word can skim the memo and grasp what it's about.

6. **Give sentences clear subjects.** If high school grammar lessons about the difference between active and passive voices left you yawning, don't despair. Just make it clear who's responsible for every action. For instance, the phrase, "once it is decided" (passive voice), leaves us asking, "Who will decide?" The quickest cure is to pin the action on a person or group. Our sample fragment becomes, "once our department decides" (which, by the way, is now in the active voice).

7. **Avoid "ramblers."** Some sentences, like this one, can be hard to read because they are so long, or because they switch subjects midway through, and by the time you reach the end of them, you may even forget what the sentence was about. Ramblers are easy to fix. Just split a long sentence into two or three shorter ones.

8. **Write the way you speak.** Contrary to popular belief, pompous language doesn't make you sound smart. It just makes you sound pompous. How many people do you know who say, "I am in receipt of" (instead of "I received"), or who refer to "utilization" (instead of "use")? Reading your memo aloud is a good way to flag such stuffy phrases.

9. **Find things to cut.** The easiest way to write concisely is not to reread every sentence as you write it. Instead, do a first draft that includes all the necessary information. Then pare it down. Throat-clearers, such as "It is important to remember that" or "It is interesting to note that," are obvious things to trim.

10. **Check for mistakes.** I'm a big fan of computerized spell-checkers, but they don't pick up words that you've *spelled* correctly but *used* incorrectly. Examples: *their* and *there*, *discreet* and *discrete*, *who's* and *whose*.

Keep in mind your busy boss or colleague who already has too much to read. Good writing will make all of your jobs easier.

Source: Deborah L. Jacobs, *San Diego Union-Tribune*, 10-23-95

B. Interpret the article. Work with your teammates to interpret the "commandments," or rules, for memo writing. Underline the key words in each rule. Use your dictionary, if necessary.

STUDENTS 1 AND 2: Interpret Rules 1–3.

STUDENTS 3 AND 4: Interpret Rules 4–6.

STUDENTS 5 AND 6: Interpret Rules 7–10.

C. Teach each other. When you **paraphrase** a passage from an article, you explain its main ideas in your own words. Explain your rules to your teammates in your own words by looking only at the words you underlined.

D. Word process it. If computers are available, type the ten commandments and make a copy. Remember: don't copy the entire article–just the commandments.

Demonstrate that you understood your teammates by writing down three of the rules for memo writing that they paraphrased. Do not look back at the article or write any of the rules that you paraphrased. Your teacher will ask certain students to write the rules they learned from their teammates on the board.

PRACTICE: **Applying the rules**

A. Revise and correct. With a partner, revise the following sentences from memos according to the advice you read.

1. Be brief (#1)

   NO: I would like to extend my congratulations for a job well done.

   YES: _____

2. Weed out repetition (#4)

   NO: In my opinion, I think there is a good chance they will respond to our offer.

   YES: _____

   _____

3. Give sentences clear subjects (#6)

   NO: Time cards must be filled out by Friday.

   YES: _____

4. Write the way you speak (#8)

   NO: We are in receipt of your recent letter concerning your account.

   YES: _____

   _____

5. Find things to cut (#9)

   NO: It is necessary that the material be received in this office by June 10.

   YES: _____

   _____

B. Diagnose the problems. In teams of two or three, review the ten rules for good memo writing. Then read the memo below. Find five problems with the memo based on these ten rules. Underline each problem and write the rule number above it. Discuss the problems with your teammates, and then work together to rewrite the memo correctly.

TO: Custodial Staff

FROM: Jim Martin

DATE: April 11, 1995

SUBJECT: Staff Meeting

There are over 15 custodians working at Southwest College. It was brought to my attention that the restrooms at the College were not clean and they were very dirty. In my personal opinion, this messiness is a bad reflection on our school and it makes all of us (the teachers, students, and community) look bad and it's not acceptable behavior. It is hoped that all custodians will attend the meeting next Thursday, April 15, to discuss the matter. Please come to the meeting with your input.

EVALUATION: **Comparing memos**

Compare your rewritten memo with one another team wrote. Talk about the similarities and differences between them. If you think something the other team wrote is better than what your team wrote, talk about why and revise your team's memo. Your teacher will ask a student from each team to read its memo aloud.

Write it up!

PREPARATION: **Interpreting and communicating**

A. Read the memos. In teams of four, take turns reading the four memos on the next two pages.

1.

Pleasure Property Management Company
2450 Broadway
Dallas, TX 75209
(214) 555-5568   FAX (214) 555-4468

TO: Alice Rodgers, Office Assistant
FROM: Mary Jo Griffith, Resident Property Manager
DATE: May 8, 1998
SUBJ: Fumigation Procedures

The fumigators will come to the property on June 15. Here are some things to do to prepare the tenants:

• Send all tenants flyers informing them of the date and time the fumigation will take place.

• Inform tenants they have to be out of their apartments for only three hours.

• Explain that all food must be taken out of kitchen cabinets.

• Advise tenants to take their pets out of the apartment during fumigation.

dp

2.

HHP ELECTRONICS
2450 Broadway
San Diego, CA 92104
(619) 555-5568   FAX (619) 555-4468

May 5, 1998

TO: Night shift lead assemblers

FR: Day shift lead assemblers

RE: Putting away equipment

Please remind your crews to put away their tools and turn off all equipment. We almost had an accident yesterday when someone noticed a soldering iron was left on all night. Also some of the tools weren't in the proper storage container. Since we all share the same equipment, please keep things as neat as possible.

CC: J. Johnson
    T. Garcia

3.

UNITED BANK
5100 Imperial Ave., Miami, FL 33196 (305) 555-2330

TO: Maintenance Crew

FROM: Debby, Toni, Ana (Front Desk)

DATE: March 12, 1998

SUBJ: Room temperature

The temperature in the lobby is extremely cold. Could you please send someone down to check the air conditioning system? We haven't taken our jackets off all week. Thanks for your assistance.

 **Microchip**

29220 Walnut Dr.
San Jose, CA 95125
(408) 555-9077
email: microchip@net.com

4.

February 4, 1998

TO: Jackie Jacobson, Night Supervisor

FR: Raymond Griffin, Technician

RE: Computer training

Could you please let me know when and where the computer class is going to be held? I missed the meeting last month when you gave the information because I was ill. Thank you for giving us the opportunity to take this class.

B. Analyze the memos. Work with your teammates to compare the memos.

STUDENT 1: Describe the similarities among the four memos.

STUDENT 2: Describe the differences among the four memos.

STUDENT 3: Was there any information in the memos you didn't understand?

STUDENT 4: Report your group's answers to the whole class.

ALL STUDENTS: Which memo do you remember the most, and why? What kind of people write memos?

C. Interpret the memos. Remain in your team of four students. Take turns reading these sentences and giving the number of the memo each one describes. A sentence may describe more than one memo. The recorder will write the letter below the correct memo on the chart.

a. The purpose is to request information.

b. The purpose is to remind employees about something.

c. This memo gives the recipient instructions on a job to do.

d. The audience is a group of custodians.

e. The letterhead includes an e-mail address.

f. The main topic is a safety concern.

g. This memo is from clerical workers.

h. A copy of this memo is going to other people.

i. This memo is asking for a response.

MEMO 1 (PAGE 171)	MEMO 2 (PAGE 171)	MEMO 3 (PAGE 172)	MEMO 4 (PAGE 172)

PRACTICE: **Writing a memo**

Imagine that you are the dean of your school. Write a memo to inform students that they can no longer eat in the classrooms. Tell them where they can eat, where they cannot eat, and when the policy goes into effect. Be sure to address all of the points mentioned in the article.

EVALUATION: **Monitor and correct your work**

After you finish writing your memo, give it to a classmate to read. Your classmate will evaluate your memo by completing this revision checklist. If you circled *no* in response to any questions, help the writer make corrections.

Classmate Revision Checklist

WRITER'S NAME: _____

CHECKER'S NAME: _____

Circle *yes* or *no*.

1. Check the content.

   ■ Did the writer inform students where they can eat? YES NO

   ■ Did the writer inform students where they cannot eat? YES NO

   ■ Did the writer say when the policy would be effective? YES NO

2. Check the expression and style.

   ■ Did the writer convey the information in a clear and effective manner? YES NO

   ■ Does the memo have a topic sentence that makes the subject clear? YES NO

   ■ Did the writer avoid repetition? YES NO

   ■ Did the writer avoid rambling? YES NO

   ■ Did the writer use a personal tone? YES NO

3. Check the grammar and spelling.

■ Are all the verbs in the correct tense?   YES NO

■ Are all words spelled correctly?   YES NO

4. Check the punctuation and capitalization.

■ Does every sentence end with a period? YES NO

■ Did the writer use capital letters where necessary? YES NO

5. Check the format.

■ Do all headings begin at the left margin? YES NO

■ Are all headings followed by colons? YES NO

■ Did the writer double-space between headings? YES NO

■ Did the writer single-space the body of the memo? YES NO

■ Did the writer double-space between paragraphs? YES NO

■ Did the writer initial the memo? YES NO

Giving instructions

When you explain a process or procedure, use the following expressions to give instructions or emphasize something important. Try using these expressions when you have something to explain to a classmate or coworker.

Make sure you . . .
Remember to . . .
Don't forget to . . .
Be careful not to . . .
It's really important that you . . .

Say it! Use these expressions to give instructions to your classmate for improving his or her memo.

A. Read for the main points. Read the information about e-mail silently and underline the main idea in each section. Then in groups of three, explain each section in your own words to each other.

What is e-mail?

E-mail (electronic mail) are messages sent from one computer to another. For example, people within companies may send interoffice messages to each other through the computer. People may also send messages to people in other companies this way. In almost every company in the United States and in many companies throughout the world, e-mail is the most common way of sending internal and cross-company correspondence.

How are memos and e-mail alike?

Both memos and e-mails are usually brief. Also, the format for e-mail is similar to the format for memos. In a memo you have to type the headings TO, FROM, and RE. In an electronic message the computer supplies these headings for you, but you must type in the specific information.

- ➤ **To:** type the e-mail address where the message is going

- ➤ **Cc:** type other e-mail addresses to which the message will be sent

- ➤ **Sub or Re:** type a brief description of the content.

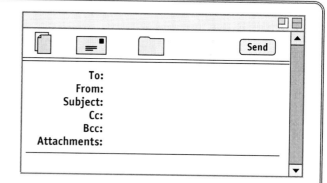

Like any other piece of writing done on the computer, e-mail may be saved and printed.

When should you use e-mail to send messages?

Use e-mail to send messages that:

- ➤ contain important information, such as the time and place of a meeting

- ➤ many people need to receive

- ➤ are urgent and need an immediate response

Do not use e-mail when:

- ➤ you are at work but your message is personal or is not related to work

- ➤ the subject of your message is emotional

- ➤ your message contains private information

- ➤ your message is of a formal nature

B. Apply what you learned. With a partner, take turns reading the following situations and decide whether you should use e-mail, telephone, send a letter, or talk face-to-face in each one. Discuss the reasons why.

1. You want to know why your teacher didn't give you a passing grade on a test. _____

2. You were interviewed for a job and you want to thank the person who interviewed you. _____

3. You forgot your medicine and you want your son to bring it to you.

   _____

4. One of your classmates wants to know what next week's homework assignment is. _____

5. You want to tell your coworker how angry you are at your boss for not giving you the day off you wanted. _____

6. You want to let everyone in the office know that the water will be turned off because of a plumbing problem. _____

7. You want to talk to your supervisor about the pay raise you were promised a few months ago. _____

8. There's going to be a staff picnic and everyone in your office is invited. _____

9. You want to find out the prices of hotels in Las Vegas because your company is having their annual business meeting there.

   _____

10. The tenant in Apartment C has paid her rent late for the past two months. You need to warn her that next time the rent is late she will have to pay a $25 late fee. _____

EVALUATION: **Share your answers**

Your teacher will call on you to read the situations aloud and explain why you chose e-mail, telephone, regular mail, or to talk face-to-face with the person.

◆ Practical grammar: Active and passive voice

Use the active voice in English when you want the listener or reader to know who or what is doing the action.

> **Anita sent** an e-mail.

The most important idea conveyed is that Anita (the subject) performed the action.

Use the passive voice when the person doing the action is not as important as what the person did.

> An e-mail **was sent** by Anita.

In fact, in some passive sentences, you don't have to mention who performed the action.

> An e-mail **was sent**.

USAGE

In most memos and business correspondence, use the active voice. Do you know the reason why? Reread the sixth "commandment" in the article and paraphrase it below:

_____

_____

_____

_____

Also use the active voice:

- ■ when you want to emphasize the subject (who did the action):

  > **Lee replaced** the front brakes.

- ■ when you speak in informal situations:

  > **The nursing assistant will take** your blood pressure.

- ■ when you want a sentence to sound more personal:

  > **Dr. Johnson wants to invite** you to an Open House.

Use the passive voice:

- when you want to emphasize what happened and not who did it:

    The letter **was typed** by the front desk clerk.
    (The important thing is that the letter got typed.)

    The **by-phrase** is used in passive sentences only when it is necessary to know who performed the action.

- when you don't know who performed the action:

    The car **was repaired**.
    The tables **were cleaned and set**.

- when, to be discreet, you want to take the emphasis off the person performing the action and put it on the action to be performed.

    The floor **should be swept**.
    All the beds **must be made** by noon.

- in scientific texts or in newspapers where the language is more formal:

    The blood sample **was analyzed and tested**.
    Hundreds of buildings **were razed** after the explosion.

FORM

Form the passive voice by using a form of the verb **be** (is, are, was, were, will be) and a past participle: (See the list of irregular past participles in the back of this book.)

SIMPLE PRESENT:	**A bonus is given** every month. **Bonuses are given** every month.
SIMPLE PAST:	**A bonus was given** last month. **Bonuses were given** last month.
SIMPLE FUTURE:	**A bonus will be given** next month. **Bonuses will be given** next month.

Look at the difference between these active and passive sentences.

ACTIVE	PASSIVE
People speak Spanish here.	**Spanish is spoken** here.
Dr. Hall invites you to his Open House.	**You are invited** to Dr. Hall's Open House.
The noise scared me.	**I was scared** by the noise.
Lee replaced the brakes.	**The brakes were replaced**.
He'll take the order.	**The order will be taken**.

Can you do it? With a partner, read the sentences below. Write **A** if the sentence is active, **P** if it is passive.

1. _____ The mailman delivered the letters.

2. _____ The car was repaired by the automotive technician.

3. _____ Children are not allowed in the building.

4. _____ The doors were locked at 6:00 P.M.

5. _____ The news of the strike surprised the employees.

6. _____ Checks are distributed by the payroll clerk.

7. _____ No employees can eat in the workrooms.

8. _____ Beverages can't be taken in the workrooms.

9. _____ The staff will not deliver your messages.

10. _____ The semester grades have already been given.

 O N L I N E !

NOTE

If you don't have a computer or cannot get on the Internet at home, you can:

1. Go to a public library near your home or school. Libraries usually have free Internet access.

2. Find out if you can get on the Internet at your school. Schools often have Internet access.

3. Ask a friend if you can use his or her computer to get on the Internet.

A. Search. For more about writing at work, look up these addresses on the Internet or search on your own:

■ Writing Center – Memo Writing:
http://www.researchpaper.com/writing_center/99.html

■ Guidelines for Writing E-mail and Usenet Messages:
http://www.earthlink.net/netfaqs/questions/NetWriting.html

B. Report. After you find the addresses, tell your classmates or write a brief paragraph about a few suggestions on writing effective memos.

A. Write. Rewrite the following memo in the active voice so that it meets the guidelines of the sixth rule of memo writing. Make it clear who is responsible for every action.

TO: Housekeepers, maintenance workers, front desk clerks
FROM: The management
DATE: December 18, 1999
RE: Daily duties

The Christmas rush is here. The hotel will be completely full for the next three weeks. Don't forget your daily duties.

Housekeeping staff: Bathrooms are cleaned first. The carpet is vacuumed late in the morning.

Maintenance: The garbage is taken out three times a day. Bulbs, wiring, and TV connections are routinely checked.

Front desk: Room numbers cannot be given to callers. Last week I made a routine room check. Towels were not left in some of the rooms. Comments were written concerning that issue in several of the rooms. Please pay attention to these details.

B. Read. When you have finished rewriting the memo, find a partner and read it aloud to him or her. Remember these basic pronunciation rules:

- Speak slowly.

- Emphasize the stressed syllables of the words.

- Your voice should go down at the end of a sentence.

EVALUATION: **Monitor and correct your work**

Compare your memo with a classmate's. Be sure the subject of every sentence is clearly stated. If your classmate's memo differs from yours, discuss the differences. Make any necessary corrections. The teacher will ask a student to read his or her memo aloud.

 # Check it!

Put a checkmark next to each activity you accomplished in this chapter.

ACADEMIC SKILLS CHECKLIST

Did you . . .

_____ write new vocabulary words in a notebook?

_____ write new grammar rules in a grammar notebook?

_____ interpret and communicate information from the article you read?

_____ acquire and evaluate data to make conclusions about the four memos?

_____ write a memo in the correct format and ask someone to revise it?

_____ revise a classmate's memo using the revision form?

_____ recognize the difference between the active and passive voice?

_____ use resources, such as a dictionary or a thesaurus, inside the classroom?

_____ use the Internet to get more information about the topic?

WORK SKILLS CHECKLIST

Did you . . .

_____ work effectively in your group? What did you do to contribute to the success of your group? _____

_____ teach someone something? What did you teach?_____ _____

_____ use a computer to type the ten rules of memo writing?

_____ decide when to use technology (e-mail) vs. a letter or other means of correspondence?

_____ use appropriate expressions to give instructions? What is one expression you used? _____

Appendix A
Irregular Verbs

SIMPLE FORM	SIMPLE PAST	PAST PARTICIPLE
be	was/were	been
beat	beat	beaten/beat
become	became	become
begin	began	begun
bend	bent	bent
bet	bet	bet
bind	bound	bound
bite	bit	bitten/bit
bleed	bled	bled
blow	blew	blown
break	broke	broken
bring	brought	brought
build	built	built
buy	bought	bought
catch	caught	caught
choose	chose	chosen
come	came	come
cost	cost	cost
creep	crept	crept
cut	cut	cut
deal	dealt	dealt
dig	dug	dug
do	did	done
draw	drew	drawn
drive	drove	driven
eat	ate	eaten
fall	fell	fallen
feed	fed	fed
feel	felt	felt
fight	fought	fought

SIMPLE FORM	SIMPLE PAST	PAST PARTICIPLE
find	found	found
fit	fit	fit
flee	fled	fled
fling	flung	flung
fly	flew	flown
forbid	forbad(e)	forbidden
forget	forgot	forgotten/forgot
forgive	forgave	forgiven
freeze	froze	frozen
get	got	gotten/got
give	gave	given
go	went	gone
grind	ground	ground
grow	grew	grown
hang	hung	hung
have	had	had
hear	heard	heard
hide	hid	hidden
hit	hit	hit
hold	held	held
hurt	hurt	hurt
keep	kept	kept
know	knew	known
lay	laid	laid
lead	led	led
leave	left	left
lend	lent	lent
let	let	let
lie	lay	lain
light	lit/lighted	lit/lighted
lose	lost	lost
make	made	made
mean	meant	meant
meet	met	met
mislay	mislaid	mislaid

SIMPLE FORM	SIMPLE PAST	PAST PARTICIPLE
mistake	mistook	mistaken
pay	paid	paid
put	put	put
quit	quit	quit
read	read	read
rid	rid	rid
ride	rode	ridden
ring	rang	rung
rise	rose	risen
run	ran	run
say	said	said
see	saw	seen
seek	sought	sought
sell	sold	sold
send	sent	sent
set	set	set
shake	shook	shaken
shed	shed	shed
shine	shone/shined	shone/shined
shoot	shot	shot
show	showed	shown/showed
shrink	shrank/shrunk	shrunk
shut	shut	shut
sing	sang	sung
sit	sat	sat
sleep	slept	slept
slide	slid	slid
speak	spoke	spoken
speed	sped	sped
spend	spent	spent
spin	spun	spun
spit	spit/spat	spit/spat
split	split	split
spread	spread	spread
spring	sprang/sprung	sprung

SIMPLE FORM	SIMPLE PAST	PAST PARTICIPLE
stand	stood	stood
steal	stole	stolen
stick	stuck	stuck
sting	stung	stung
stink	stank/stunk	stunk
strike	struck	struck/stricken
string	strung	strung
strive	strove	striven
swear	swore	sworn
sweep	swept	swept
swim	swam	swum
swing	swung	swung
take	took	taken
teach	taught	taught
tear	tore	torn
tell	told	told
think	thought	thought
throw	threw	thrown
understand	understood	understood
upset	upset	upset
wake	woke/waked	waked/woken
wear	wore	worn
weave	wove	woven
weep	wept	wept
win	won	won
wind	wound	wound
withdraw	withdrew	withdrawn
wring	wrung	wrung
write	wrote	written

Appendix B
Dictation Key

1. What Are Employers Looking For?

Have you ever used the classified advertisements from the newspaper to help you find a job? These ads describe qualifications for employment. Many businesses are looking for the same qualities: workers who are organized, motivated, and qualified for the position.

2. Building Self-Confidence

The article you are going to read is about increasing your self-confidence. The article suggests that you can improve self-confidence by:

- setting realistic goals
- studying
- welcoming change

3. Volunteering: On-the-Job Training

Have you ever volunteered in your child's school or at church? Volunteering sharpens your skills and gives you confidence. It's an excellent way to help others and meet people who might help you find employment later.

4. Effective Job Applications

Your job application represents you. A neat, organized, and complete form tells an employer a lot about you. A messy, unorganized, and incomplete application gives an employer doubts about your job performance.

5. Successful Job Interviews

Getting an interviewer to like you is essential if you want to get the job. The article you'll read is about how to give an interviewer a good first impression. Being friendly, energetic, and enthusiastic will help you land a job.

6. **Small Talk at the Water Cooler**

   Joan has worked as a data entry clerk at a large company downtown for two weeks. There are about 15 other clerical workers on her floor. She wants to get acquainted with the other employees but she doesn't know how. What should she say? How will she start a conversation?

7. **Improving Relationships at Work**

   Most of you have worked or studied with someone who had a habit that bothered you. What should you do about it? Some people think you ought to tell the person directly. Other people would rather avoid the confrontation and suffer in silence.

8. **Handling Criticism**

   The office manager asked Melissa to file all the patients' charts as soon as possible. A few hours later, she noticed that the charts were still on Melissa's desk. Didn't Melissa understand her directions? Why didn't she file the charts?

9. **Having a Positive Attitude**

   George hired Ernie to work in his garage as an automotive technician. Ernie works hard and has excellent skills. The problem is that nobody wants to work with him because he's usually in a bad mood. The customers also complain about his attitude. They say he doesn't have the patience to answer their questions. George doesn't know what to do.

10. **Writing at Work**

    A memo is a form of internal correspondence that people in companies write. Memos provide written records of conversations, meetings or decisions. Another form of correspondence is electronic mail, or e-mail. In many companies, people send interoffice messages through the computer. A company can link all of its employees from any location by a computer.